LIFE:

In All It's Fullness

A Festschrift

PRESENTED TO HONOUR

Rev. D. S. Jeevan Babu

For his 60 years of Life,
33 years of Pastoral Ministry and
31 years of Married Life

ii

LIFE:

In All It's Fullness

A Festschrift

PRESENTED TO HONOUR

Rev. D. S. Jeevan Babu

For his 60 years of Life,
33 years of Pastoral Ministry and
31 years of Married Life

EDITED BY

Kiran and Keerthi

ISPCK
2009

Life: In All It's Fullness – Published by the Rev. Dr. Ashish Amos of the Indian Society for Promoting Christian Knowledge (ISPCK), Post Box 1585, 1654, Madarsa Road, Kashmere Gate, Delhi-110006.

ISBN : 978-81-8458-095-2

Laser typeset by **ISPCK,** Post Box 1585, 1654, Madarsa Road, Kashmere Gate, Delhi-110006.
Tel: 23866323 / 22
e-mail– ashish@ispck.org.in • ella@ispck.org.in
website-www.ispck.org.in

Contents

vi

Foreword

I am happy to write this foreword for the book entitled "Life in all its fullness" – a Festschrift brought out to celebrate the 60th birthday of Rev. D.S. Jeevan Babu, a presbyter working in the Karnataka Central Diocese of the Church of South India.

Rev. Jeevan Babu is a faithful servant of God and has held important posts in the Diocese as well as outside the diocese. He is a soft spoken person and one exceptional quality in him is he never hurts the feelings of anyone even if his own feelings are hurt. He is deeply committed to the pastoral ministry. His strength in the pastoral ministry are his visits to those who are sick- not just physical ailments, but also that of counselling those who are troubled and motivating his congregation members to be involved in the ministry and mission. To say the least, we are proud of his pastoral ministry in the Diocese. Jeevan also has sense of wry humour that puts flavour into all that he does.

This Festschrift can be divided into two parts- the first part being a biographical sketch. Jeevan when translated means life and Jeevan emphatically portrays that his life is a gift from God. On two occasions when death almost claimed him, Jeevan affirms that it is God who saved him and that God has a purpose in his life – the purpose is that Jeevan not only should lead a good and happy family life but also most importantly he be a good pastor, always being concerned about the well-being of those who are committed to his care in the pastoral ministry. This he feels is living life in all its fullness.

The second part consists of articles written in honour of Jeevan. All the contributors in this book are people who are or have been associated with Jeevan in some way or the other.

Since the topics of discussion vary from person to person around the theme "fullness of life" their perspective obviously is also varied. However, one can discern the common thread woven through all the articles. A theologian like Rev. Dr. K.C. Abraham begins by saying "Life is God's precious gift, it is to be preserved and enhanced." He goes further to state that life is to be lived not only individually being committed to God, life in its fullness can be realized only when this life is shared and particularly with the less fortunate ones in the society. In order to share this life with others one has to undergo a fundamental change in his/ her life which is 'metanoia'. Further, one must reject exclusivism and accept plurality in order to share this life in fullness.

A scientist like Dr. G.S.D Babu looks at creation from his background as a scientist. He arrives at the conclusion that the grandeur of the Universe is governed by the laws of nature. All scientists have been doing is to discover the latent principles underlying the laws of nature, but God is the originator of the laws of nature. Therefore science and religion are not contradictory to one another instead they complement each other.

Bishop Surya Prakash affirms that the fullness of life for an individual is possible only when he/she is deeply rooted in Christ. But this fullness of life needs to be expressed in terms of the service to society and particularly to the needy and the downtrodden.

Dr. Moses Manohar states that in order to achieve fullness of life one has to be imbibed with values- practicing values like forgiveness and promoting equality among all, expressing solidarity with all those who live on the periphery of society.

Dr. Ipe Joseph is of the opinion that values need to be instilled in the children from a very young age and this should be through the medium of Christian education. In this process the role of the parents, Sunday school teachers, day school scripture teachers, evangelists and pastors play an important role in moulding the character of the children.

Rev. Y. Moses is of the opinion that fullness of life is not the prerogative of those who are rich in material comforts nor is it the prerogative of those who have nothing, but it belongs to those who do God's will. Hence one needs to learn to reject his/her preoccupations with one's own special, personal or group interest and turn towards the interest of others.

Bishop Geevarghese Mar Coorilos states that this fullness of life cannot be complete if it does not involve the whole universe and eco-justice and eco-spirituality needs to be taken seriously.

Mrs. Porkodi Prabhakaran states that even though there are number of laws enacted in India to empower human beings to lead a fuller life, this life has not been realized since human beings to implement these laws are not faithful. Therefore she recommends that fuller life is possible only when one is in Christ and honours God and the State for the cause of fullness of life for others.

This volume is edited by Kiran and Keerthi, son and daughter of Rev. Jeevan Babu. I congratulate their efforts in bringing out this volume. Since this is their maiden venture in editing a book finer nuance of editing, proof reading, spell check, page setting and layout etc., needs to be fine tuned. Despite all this the book is an expression of their love, respect and devotion to their father – it is a labour of love. It is my prayer that this Festschrift may inspire its readers to be more committed to God and thereby experience fullness of life not only on a personal level, but also that through the individual this fullness of life can be extended to others as well.

– **Rt. Rev. S. Vasanthakumar**
Bishop
Karnataka Central Diocese

x

Family Acknowledgements

We, the members of the family sincerely acknowledge our thanks to God for making it possible to have this thanksgiving festschrift to honour Rev. D. S. Jeevan Babu. We specially thank Rt. Rev. Dr. Surya Prakash, Bishop in CSI Karimnagar Diocese, His Grace Geevergese Mar Coorlose Bishop of Jacobite Syrian Orthodox Church, Rev. Dr. Ipe Joseph, General Sercretary, All India Sunday School Union, Dr. K. C. Abraham a renowned Indian theologian, Dr. Moses Manohar, Director ICSA, Chennai, Rev. Dr. Y. Moses, Freelance NGO, Mrs. Porkodi Prabhakaran, Principal, Bishop Cotton Women's Christian Law College, Bangalore, Dr. G. S. D. Babu, Scientist, Birla Institute of Fundamental Research, Mr. John Zachariah, Principal of Cathedral High School and College, Bangalore. Our special thanks to ISPCK for publishing this material. We owe our gratitude to Rt. Rev. Vasanthakumar for writing the foreword to this book. We also thank Mrs. Jothi Priya and Mr. Jerald for giving a beautiful shape to this book.

We are very sure this festschrift will not only give you deeper insight into Rev. Jeevan Babu's life and ministry but also life in general. Please do remember Rev. Jeevan Babu and his ministry in your prayers.

– **Kiran and Keerthi**
Son and Daughter of
Rev. D. S. Jeevan Babu

Rev. D.S. Jeevan Babu

(*A brief profile*)

Devavaram Samuel Jeevan Babu, son of Mrs. Padma Yesupadam and Late. Mr. Yesupadam, was born in Madanapalle in Andhra Pradesh on 20th January 1949, true to his name he is a real gift to the church. He comes to us with rich experience and deep spirituality, a search which began in 1972 in the United Theological College where he completed his B.D. after about 12 years he proceeded to South Korea to take M.Th Degree in Missions from reputed Presbyterian Theological Seminary and College, Seoul, South Korea. He was ordained as a Deacon at Central Church, Vellore in 1976 and presbyter in 1977.

In his ministry, which spanned for over 33 years, Rev. Jeevan Babu has served in various capacities. He has been a Presbyter and a Manager of a Boarding home and in crèche homes in rural areas in Vellore Diocese. He was then invited to be Registrar at the United Theological College. During this time he had an opportunity to produce radio programmes at FEBA.

He was then invited to be the presbyter of Telugu churches in Karnataka Central Diocese. He held several positions in the diocese such as the editor of the diocesan newsletter and, later on he was elected as the associate treasurer of the diocese and served as the director of the youth and communication departments and convener of the Ministerial Committee of the Karnataka central dioceses.

There was an invitation from NCCI to be the Secretary for Mission and Evangelism, which was accepted by him and was deputed by the diocese for five years to serve in the NCCI. During these five years he held many responsibilities as Secretary for Projects and Secretary for Ecumenism and Dialogue and the Editor of the Newsletter and NCCI review. As the Executive Secretary his involvement and contribution in the World Council of Churches (WCC), Christian Conference of Asia (CCA), Council for world mission (CWM) and many other international conferences has been widely recognized and acknowledged.

A person with deep conviction in a new spirituality of prayer and preaching, Rev. Jeevan Babu is a pastor par excellence. He passionately loves pastoral life. His preaching has been most admired, thought provoking and controversial to traditional churchgoer. He has authored many books in English and Telugu that were published by leading publishing houses in India.

Rev. Jeevan Babu widely travelled both within the country and outside. He has attended several international conferences and consultations in many continents of the world. Endowed with a rare musical gift, Rev. Jeevan Babu brings into his spirituality a unique combination of music, prayer and worship. As a human being he enjoys fellowship of all people irrespective of creed and colour. He has always been sensitive to the needs of others and above all has strived hard to be a good human being.

At the NCCI leaders of various churches in India have always looked upto Rev. Jeevan Babu for leadership, inspiration, creativity and intercession. Jeevan Babu's heart is where the congregation is. We are sure that CSI will be highly enriched with his creativity and commitment even in the days to come. The church would continue to experience a new spirituality, always relating to the context of poverty, discrimination and exclusion, which are close to Jeevan Babu's heart. We wish Rev. Jeevan Babu, Mrs. Kasthuri, Kiran and Keerthi God's guidance, blessings and the guidance of the Holy spirit that he may continue to enrich people's life, inspire individuals and above all establish the kingdom values of love, peace, justice, and integrity of creation.

Educational Qualifications

Rev. Jeevan Babu passed SSLC in 1965 from Madanapalle Hope High School. He did his B.Com in 1969 at Besent Theosophical College of Sri. Venkateshwara University. He completed his B.D in 1976 in Bangalore at United Theological College of Serampore University. He did his M.Th in missions at Presbyterian Theological Seminary & College in Seoul in South Korea in 1988.

He was ordained at CSI Deacon in Vellore in 1976 and as a presbyter in 1977 in Vellore. His thesis in B.D was on "The Ordination of women with special reference to CSI". The thesis for M.Th was on "A Theology of mission with implications to the local congregations in CSI".

Ministerial Responsibilities

Presbyter in Chittoor, Vellore Diocese – 1976 – 79

Manager, Beattee Hostel, Chittoor – 1976 – 79

Manager, 2 Crèche Homes in rural areas – 1976 – 79

Registrar at United Theological College, Bangalore – 1979 – 81

Producer of Radio programme for FEBA in Telugu for youth Hon 1980 – 84

Presbyter of 3 Telugu congregations and one English speaking congregation at Kolar Gold fields – 1981 – 86

Editor of the Diocesan news letter – 1985 – 86

Associate Treasurer for the diocese – 1985 – 87

St. John's Church in Bangalore – 1986 – 1987

St. Peter's Telugu Church, 1987

Convenor, Ministrial committee CSI – KCD – 1987, 1991- 1993, 2002 - 2007

Director of youth and communications in Karnataka Central Diocese – 1993 - 94

All Saints Church – 1989 - 1994

Deputed to NCCI – 1994 - 1999
  Secretary for Mission and Evangelism
  Secretary for Projects and National Screening Board – India
  Secretary for Ecumenism and Dialogue
  Editor NCCI News letter and NCC Review

Presbyter, St. John's Church, Fort, Vellore – 1999-2000

St. Peter's Telugu Church, Bangalore – 2000 – 2005

Holy Cross Church, Jalahalli – 2005 – 2006

St. Matthew's Church, Bangalore – 2006 – till date.

Book Published

Andamaina Jeevitham (Telugu)   - 1986

Amazing Life (sets of poems in English) – 1992

Celebrating Family Life – 1994

Positive Approach to Church Politics – 1995

Mission Hermeneutics – 1995

Mission to Cities – 1996

Lectionary of our Times – 1996

India's report on Gospel & Culture (an Indian encounter) – 1996

Praxis Oriented Lent – 1997

The Signpost – 1997

Transforming the Church in India – 1998

God of God – 1998

Who are these Christians in India - 1998

Peace – 2000

Prayers Not for Sale –2004

Know Marriage, No Divorce –2005

Gun or God –2006

Images – 2007

Mission – 2008

Articles Written for National Council of Churches Review

Family Sunday liturgy

National celebration

Gospel and Culture

Make things happen

Ye Hai Democracy (Editorial)

Is Jesus alive today (Editorial)

A tribute to Dietrich Bonhoeffer

In Christ today (Editorial)

Celebration

Local congregation

Patriotic poems

Independence Day liturgy

Human Rights and You (Editorial)

Celebrating Womankind

M.M. Thomas Festschrift – mission statement

Bible Studies

The Church

The Mission of the Church

Book of James
Roman 12
Review, repentance, and renewal

Articles Published in the International Magazines

Interlit – poem
International Review in Mission
Evangelism – Indian Encounter
WCC Letter on Evangelism

People's Reporter

❖ Ordained for what?

❖ A Dalit's cry

❖ A tribute to Dietrich Bonehoffer

❖ Reflections – Pokhran

❖ Today's Youth for Tomorrow's Church – CSI Golden Jubilee Book

❖ Incarnation of Christ in a Pluralistic World: South India churchman

❖ Communications for Liberation: South India Churchman

❖ CSI Yesterday, Today and Tomorrow: South India churchman

❖ Power, Principles and People: South India Churchman

❖ Lent 2001: South India Churchman

Major International Conferences Attended

❖ England, Ireland and India NCCI Conference, Haryana

❖ Common Witness Conference (WCC), (Philippines)

❖ Re-reading the Bible (CCA), Bangkok

* Decade against Violence (WCC), Bossey, Switzerland
* Common Witness (WCC), Bossey, Switzerland
* World Mission Conference, (WCC), Salvador, Brazil
* Visit to NCCI, New York and California
* World Council of Churches Assembly, Zimbabwe

We the congregation of St. Matthew's Church and the pastorate committee congratulate our presbyter – in – charge Rev. Jeevan Babu on this 60th birthday and may God bless him and his family.

Rev. D. S. Jeevan Babu is presbyter - in - charge of St. Matthew's Church from 2006. He is one of the seniormost Pastors from C S I - K.C D. If one goes by his past life it clearly indicates that God was with him all along. God has chosen him before he could be even conceived.

He came through a very simple and a difficult life. God chose him to be his servant and he obeyed. God made him gain experience working, in villages, in towns, in small organizations, in big organizations, in many states in India and even abroad too. He has been blessed with a God fearing and loving wife, children, mother, brothers and sisters.

These days it is too difficult for a pastor to manage a church and the same way it is too difficult for the congregation to get along with a Presbyter - in charge. Thank God for having given the same frequency of thoughts for the congregation of St. Matthew's Church and our pastor Rev. Jeevan Babu.

There are many things one can appreciate about Rev. Jeevan Babu. Let me share few of his good qualities which has impressed me the most.

Whenever the church was in crucial situations he has taken decisions which never was partial, selfish, hurting or against the interest of the church. He is very found of introducing new things in all walks of time. Some of his ideas were revolutionary. Whenever there is a thing to be appreciated whoever it may be he would make it a point to appreciate with a word of encouragement. He has never used the church pulpit and preaching for hurting anyone or for any selfish reasons. His commitment to the church is commendable. He never misses any of the Sunday worships and any congregational functions. He is very time conscious and always there half an hour in advance. He is a peace lover and would go to any extent to maintain peace. All these habits of Rev. Jeevan Babu and the wisdom he enjoys goes to prove beyond doubts that God is with him and leading him.

We the congregation of St. Matthew's church believe that Rev. Jeevan Babu has been given to us as a gift of God.

We pray to God to give him healing , good health, long life and peace. May God bless his family with peace, joy and happiness. May his tribe increase.

– **E.Vijayan**
Secretary
St. Matthew's Church

1. Sweet Sixty Memories

☆ I was born on 20th January, 1949. Doctors pronounced that I would not live more than 24 hours. They had informed my father who was in the military. My mother knelt down and prayed to God to save me. Today is 20th Jan., 2009. I have completed sixty spring seasons in my life. Every year I keep celebrating my birthday to tell people that it is God who is behind my life from day one and is still using me in his ministry.

☆ I was around 7 to 9 months old. My mother made me sleep outside the house and after she had eaten her food she came out to throw water and to her shock, she saw a black cobra crawling on my stomach. My family was surprised that the snake did not harm me. My mother thanked God for this miracle.

☆ There was a Christmas programme in Hope Hostel in Madanapalle, where I was an inmate of the hostel for 7 years, as the Chief Guest started preaching, he referred to many biblical passages in his sermon. We were asked to read the Bible verses. I read all those passages correctly. I myself marveled how I could quickly take those portions from the Bible and read it before anybody could get on to those passages. At the end, the Chief Guest asked, 'who is that boy who read all those passages, come to the stage'. Hesitantly, I went up to the stage and he gave me Re.1/- as a gift. I refused at the first instance, as my mother told me not to accept anything like that if anybody offers to me. Then our warden insisted that I should take, and hence, I accepted. I was the happiest boy that day. It was certainly God's intervention in my life.

✰ When I was studying in 8th standard, I went to Arogyavaram where my grandmother stayed. There was a big well near our place. All the boys were swimming. Somebody invited me too to learn swimming. That was a very deep well. I was just standing at the edge of well for my turn to learn. Then, suddenly, an elderly boy came to me shouting "Aye, Babu, why are you standing there? Come on, jump, I will teach you." I told him, I do not know swimming and I was waiting for my brother to come up so that I can use the necessary things to learn." He did not listen to me properly as he was drunk. He lifted me up and threw me down in the well. I was struggling in the well not knowing swimming and everybody was shouting at that man who threw me into the well. Somehow, having seen me struggling in the well, the others who knew swimming jumped down and pulled me up. I survived. Another beautiful intervention of God in my life. I started realizing that God has a purpose in saving me from that danger.

✰ It was in class one, My teacher asked me, to 'act as Valmiki Maharshi.' I, did it. It was an unforgettable scene in my mind. My acting career started in me.

✰ It was in those days when I went to a school in Chintakayala veedhi in Tirupathi. Our teacher was so much impressed about my knowledge of alphabets. I was asked to sit next to my teacher in class. I still remember, I was so happy about it.

✰ It was in 8th standard or so, that I was elected as the CE (Christian Endeavour) secretary. I was so excited about it as I had to conduct CE prayer meetings every Sunday evening.

✰ I still remember that I had to stand in the first line to lead the hostel students though I was in l0th standard, both to school and the church since I was short and I loved to be in the front to lead the hostlers.

★ Around the time while studying in 9th standard or so, I won the second prize in Music competition in the school for playing the Mouth Organ. Even before this time, I started picking up interest in singing.

★ One of the saddest days in my life was when I failed in 10th standard. My fathers' scoldings put me to a great shame. This failure challenged me to work hard in studies. Not that I was lazy. Somehow things were not going into my head. This one failure helped me to go up to Master of Theological Studies without any further failure.

★ One thing I cannot forget in my life, is the beatings I received with cane for failing in Telugu paper in 9th standard by our Hostel warden. He made all failures to gather in the dining hall and one by one he would beat the boys. Sometimes, we ran around escaping the beatings and he used to chase us and beat. Many times, many of us used to wet our pants while receiving the beatings.

★ Once, my warden went out for shopping, and he asked us not to play in the ground. As soon as he left, all of us went out in the ground and played Hockey with temporarily made hockey sticks. While playing, I received a blow near my eye. As soon as he came back, my colleagues reported to the warden. He simply said, "'let it be', I asked you all not to play'". I felt so bad, but realized my mistake of disobeying.

★ I remember, when I was studying in 5th standard in a village called Pallam, my teacher asked a question, and none of my classmates answered, but, I answered. Then, my teacher asked me to slap all the students. Though I slapped every-body very softly. But when I came to slap the girls, I felt very bad.

★ When I was in 10th standard, two of my classmates (girls) used to come to my class during the interval and give me some eatables. I cannot forget their concern for me.

✪ When I was in the Hope Hostel, Madanapalle, I participated in almost all the programmes of the Hostel. I used to be after our warden, Mr. Walton Jeremiah pleading him to put me in the group for both drama and singing. I am proud to say that I sang almost all his songs first time. It was here and my association with him, I picked up singing and also little bit of writing.

✪ While I was in the hostel, I used to accompany a group of my hostelmates to go to evangelistic camps to the surrounding villages. I simply used to enjoy these trips. We the hostellers were invited to go and sing the whole night at the death of any church members. We all felt it as a privilege and not as a burden.

✪ I was so privileged to have been invited to be the Chief Guest at the centenary celebrations of Hope High School, Madanapalle, after I completed my graduation and ordination as Presbyter.

✪ My father was the only breadwinner. I remember, when I was studying in the high school for one year, I was a day scholar. We were five brothers and two sisters at that time. One day had to go to school without food. Somewhere in the house I found a small coin and I took that and brought jaggery and went to school. There my master beat me and insulted me for not having a thakli with which we make thread out of cotton. For a few days during that month our family went through a lot of difficulties. During those days, my father fell sick and was admitted in the hospital. The sexton of the church even rang deathknell announcing the death of my father, though he was alive.

✪ I studied my PUC and B.Com in Madanapalle as a day scholar. We lived in the police lines. My father used to tell me, 'see, you are a Christian, and should do well in studies compared to other religious people.'

✪ While I was in the college, I was elected as the President of the local SCM, which was attached to the local church. As a SCM President I brought my colleagues to Bangalore

SCM headquarters for a retreat. We had an unforgettable experience with Mr. Karat. This SCM experience gave us little courage to speak in English and laid a foundation for leadership.

☆ When I was studying B.Com, first year, one of my friends came up to me and said, 'I have given your name for sports as a junior athlete'. Till that time, I had never participated in any sports events. With hesitance, I went to the ground and participated in five events and won the first prize in all the events such as 100 meters, 400 meters and 800 meters running race, high jump and long jump and I became a junior champion without any previous experience. The following year also, I was the champion. I could not win the third time.

☆ I remember very well the way I studied during my B.Com. I used to go regularly to the nearby paddy fields and read loudly. During the night, I used sit under the streetlights for my study without any grumbling.

☆ I also remember during one of the exams I had taken a tablet for my sickness. Having sat on the floor for hours together, I got a boil on my back. With blood oozing from that wound, I went for my exams and came out with flying colours. In those days, every year the university conducted exam. They used to publish results in the newspapers.

☆ When the final year exams results were published, I ran to tell my father that I got through my final year in B. Com. My father gave me one rupee and told me to go and enjoy a film. I had nice tea and went home to tell my mother and others in the police lines. I asked my father to send me for M. Com, but my father told me, "that you have six brothers and sisters. How can I manage to send you for higher studies." Then came my search for a job. I found a job in a private finance corporation with a salary of Rs 50/- per month.

☆ As I was looking for a better job, I got an interview call for SSB selection from Mysore. It was great experience during this interview. I went through all the tests somewhat satisfactorily. None of the people who went there were selected. We all called them as Rejection board and came back to our home. Quite an experience. It was for the first time that I took a train journey all alone. And for the first time I had experienced such a disciplined five-day interview.

✪ As soon as I got my B.Com results, my father took me to our pastor and requested him to recommend me for theological study. He immediately looked at me, almost looked down upon me, he was so tall and I was so short, and he told me, "You want to do theology? I don't think you will be able to." Look for some other job. He discouraged us very much. It was at this time I was challenged and decided to pursue my theological study and was waiting for an opportunity.

✪ Then, I went for an interview for the post of wardens for the hostels run by KNH. After the interview, they said that they would be appointing me as a clerk at the Head office of Rayalseema Diocese in Cuddapah, under two missionaries. Miss P.B. Hockings and Miss Beatty Williams. This experience being in Cuddapah under two missionaries gave me a rich experience in discipline and in English.

✪ I was a little romantic person. So I used to write letters to my girlfriend. She used to write beautiful Telugu and I responded in the same way. I improved my literary capacity through her. One day, my father visited me in Cuddapah when I was in the office, He went through some books in my room and found a letter, which he went through, and silently went home and reported to my mother. My mother politely called me and warned me. This incident reduced my frequency of writing letters. After a few months, I got a letter from her saying that she married her brother-in-law.

✪ My father had sent me a letter saying that in Chittoor church they have announced the need for Telugu speaking pastors and Bishop Henry Lazarus asked my dad to apply for me. And he applied on behalf of me.

✰ Within a few days, after I received this letter, I received a letter of Bishop Lesslie Newbegin from Madras diocese inviting me to come for the interview. I was so excited. I was helped by the local pastor of a Telugu Church and the Area chairman. I cannot forget the interview with Bishop Lesslie Newbegin. After the interview he offered me a cup of coffee. It was a big honour for me. Certainly, it was God's call for me. The Bishop straight away recommended me to UTC.

✰ I could not do well in the entrance test at UTC. I was not upto their standard. They gave me a second chance. At that time I was still in Cuddapah. Bishop L. V. Azariah gave me coaching in English grammar. I was so happy to see in the question paper the same passage the Bishop had asked me to work on. I passed the entrance test.

✰ In Cuddapah, they had arranged for a farewell for me. The same pastor who refused me, had to say a few words. He said, "You should have gone through us." I replied in my thanks speech, "I did ask you to, but you refused me." I cannot forget this meeting.

✰ I cannot forget the warm welcome I received from the two Telugu ladies i.e., Florence and Abraham Akka in UTC Bangalore. Of course, then, the day followed by raging of freshers which was very new for me. After raging the way my seniors loved me was so much that I never felt lonely. After preaching my first sermon in the chapel, one my senior student lifted me up for that sermon.

✰ One thing which I cannot forget during my UTC life was the election to the Carey Society Secretary' post. All Telugu people had proposed my name. It was almost unanimous. But later, somebody's name was proposed from another language group. But I won the election. That night, myself and my friend who contested and some other friends together went for a cup of tea.

✰ After the first three months of Greek, I came for Christmas holidays just to see my father who was sick in bed. Doctors almost pronounced that he is going to die soon. I did not believe and I was preparing to go back to UTC after the holidays. My father was taken to Palamaner, which is his native place. From there my mother sent a word saying that my father would like to meet me. All the relatives arrived. One day before his death, he called me and asked me to bend down on him, and told me, you have to continue your theological study and serve the people as pastor. You will see many deaths like my death. Only if you work as a pastor I will have salvation. I handover your mother and all your brothers and sisters in your hands'. He became silent after words. On 13th January, 1973 early in the morning when everybody was sleeping except my grandmother and me, he breathed his last. My fathers' words of his wish gave me a lot of strength to go to UTC. At that time none of us were earning. God indeed took care of my mother and six brothers and sisters.

★ As soon as I came to college after my father' death our college elected me as the auditor of the hostel. After going through the accounts I recommended that students could run the hostel mess than giving it for contract to somebody else. Ever since that day till today the students run the mess.

★ My life in UTC days was very transforming. From an evangelical outlook, I changed to be a very liberal theologian. I never regret this change. I had the best of teachers for every subject. My Greek teacher was Dr. Herald K. Mountain, the author of Greek Lexicon, my Hebrew teachers were Dr. Mayer and Dr. E. C. John. My theology teachers were Dr. Christopher Duraisingh and Dr. Russel Chandran and Rev. Dr. A. P. Nirmal. Dr. Somen Dass was my Ethics teacher and my Tutor was Rev. Dr. Mike Butterworth.

★ I strongly believe that I had spent my formative years in UTC. Every year I participated in the college play. In the play 'the cup of trembling' the life story of Detrich Bonnehoffer I acted as junior Bonnehoffer, who was a famous Christian leader in Germany whom I like very much. After the play one girl came and hugged me, which

I cannot forget and also Rev. Dr. Frank Collison came and appreciated me so much for my acting.

★ At the farewell party for the final year students myself and another friend of my class did a skit. In that skit I had acted as a pregnant lady. I had to remove my mush also. It was a very hilarious skit. Next day in the morning Dr. Chandran noticed my mushless face and he said, 'Was that you', and laughed.

★ Though Madras Diocese had sponsored me for theological studies I was asked to go to Vellore diocese, since diocese was bifurcated and the need for Telugu pastors are more in Vellore area. I was posted to Chittoor, particularly to take care of the village pastorate. In the first pastorate committee meeting some members insisted me to stay in the village where there were no facilities. I had to argue with them and they were also very much argumentative and were little harsher than me. That was big shock for me. I came home weeping. Believe it or not, the whole night I kept on weeping. Early morning, I had to go to a village. Even in the bus I was in tears. As soon as I reached the village the leader of the village brought a big tender coconut which was so tasty. Seeing their love, I regained my strength. As I was travelling in the bus an image of the Cross came to my mind and comforted me. 'Your sufferings are nothing before my suffering. Your suffering are due to your pride.' This image in my mind made me forget that first meeting with the Pastorate committee. I enjoyed going to the village by bus and by my cycle. In rural areas you really experience genuine love and respect and you will feel satisfied with your ministry.

★ Then the talk of the town was about my marriage. I loved a Telugu girl at that time. One day her uncle came to see me. After spending few minutes in our house they left home, and I got a message from him saying that they were not interested in me for the only reason that I had long hair. I felt very bad about their decision and the girl was not able to convince her parents. As I was teaching the confirmation class I found another girl. We spoke to her parents and they agreed. Then one day, her uncle came to see me and he sent me a word saying that they are not interested though the mother and the girl agreed for. I felt very bad, again. Then came the real one, Kasthuri from Bangalore through my uncle Rev. C. Peter. Through reliable sources I was told that she was a Sunday school teacher. Without any hesitation, I said yes.

☆ On 15th May, 1978 we both accepted each other as life partners in the Town Church, Chittoor. I cannot forget the help rendered by Miss. Suguna Devasundaram, Mr. Barnabass, Mr. B. A. David and Mr. Daniel Jayaraj. Each of them put Rs.250/- and my grandmother, Mrs. Jayamma Peter gave me Rs.1000/-. My congregation members from Keenattam Palli sent a bag of rice. That's all. The marriage was over. Kasthuri came into our family as a great gift of God to me.

☆ I started with two crèche homes in two villages and I was also made incharge of the Beattie Hostel in Chittoor. The diocese gave me charge of Chittoor church, Pakala Church and around 15 village churches around Chittoor. I gladly ministered to all these churches. I was very much blessed.

☆ I came to know that UTC was looking for someone, to be the Registrar. I applied, and got it. I enjoyed serving UTC as the Registrar. I lost my first son during that time and I was planning to call him as Kranthi, which means revolution. I was upset at that time. Everybody told me to go back to Pastoral ministry. I did not get a favourable response from Vellore diocese. Dr. Chandran was the moderator' commissary at Karnataka central Diocese and also the principal of UTC. He gave me relieving orders from UTC and at the same time gave me an appointment order to join the Karnataka Central Diocese. I was appointed for 3 Telugu congregations, one English Speaking congregation in KGF. I was very sure that it was God's plan for me to come back to pastoral ministry. Ministry at KGF was satisfying and enriching.

☆ One of the congregation members scolded me very badly in front of the congregation. I knew he was misguided by somebody. I was in tears. The same day I told my wife that we would go to his house and reconcile. As soon as he saw me he wept aloud, and we both wept together. He asked for my forgiveness. This event is the most unforgettable event of my life in KGF.

☆ Kiran was born in KGF hospital on 5th Jan., 1982. Our expenses for that day were only Rs.50/-. Kasthuri did not leave her job because it was a government approved job. She used to come for holidays and during the weekends to be with us. I never used to leave KGF except for some special meetings in the diocese. Keerthi was born on 26th Oct., 1985 at 5:00 am. As soon as she was born she did not cry. I waited and prayed to God and at 7:00 am. the news came that everything was all right. She cried, and I heard her crying. I sincerely thanked God for the miracle that happened.

☆ In those days my friends at KCD asked me to contest as the Treasurer of the Diocese. I did not know many people in the Diocese. I never asked anybody to vote for me. My friends went for the campaign and I had to contest against a more popular and senior person. I won the election. I served the diocese as Associated Treasurer for two years.

☆ While I was in KGF, on one of the Harvest festival worship services as I was preparing my sermon. I wanted to preach on tithing. I was not paying tithe till that day. I said to my-self, 'I have to pay my tithes, only then I should preach.' That was the first time I paid 65 rupees with a lot of thinking in my mind on how to survive with less money for myself and all the family members, my mother and other six brothers and sisters were with me and my wife. I decided, and offered my tithes. From then on, I never looked back. As soon I receive my salary I first keep my tithes apart, then only, I spend my rest of the salary till day. I never had any financial problem. I was able to save enough and thank God.

☆ As I completed my five-year term I was transferred to St. John's Church, Bangalore. Since I was working among the miners in KGF, I never used to wear good dress and shoes to identify with my church members. When I entered St. John's Church somebody cautioned, 'you cannot walk around the church with sandals on. You should always wear shoes.' After a few days, one of our pastors told me seeing my dress, 'Aye Jeevan, you look very civilized now'!

✮ After a year I was transferred to St. Peter's Telugu Church. While I was there I got a letter from the Presbyterian Theological College and Seminary, Seoul, Korea saying that I got admission to M.Th in Third World theology with scholarship and travel benefits. Another thankful day to God for me. Immediately the Diocese relieved me and I reached Korea and my teacher came to receive me and carried my box. On one side, I was feeling very bad to leave my small children, on the other hand I was so thankful to God for this opportunity. Leadership was always behind me. I was elected as the President of Third World Students Center. We were 25 foreigners under the principleship of Dr. Kim Yong Bock. Only once in a month I used to contact my family members through letters, as we did not have a phone. I enjoyed my studies and ministry in Korea. I even enjoyed minus 18 degrees temperature during winter. I had a group of lovely Korean students who used to come to me and sometimes take me around for Bible studies and learning the English language. I cannot forget my travel to Cheju Islands near Japan where most of the occupants were war-victim widows. It is also a place for honeymoon for the newly weds. Meanwhile, the Japanese were exploiting women. In this place there are churches especially for war-victim-widows. They also pay tithes for the church. I had wonderful experiences visiting churches and important places of interest. Once I participated in Easter service held on the old airport. Around one million people gathered and after the service there was not even a single bit of paper or anything in the place. I saw everybody picking up waste papers and so on. I was also privileged to go upto the borderline between South and North Korea.

★ After spending one and a half year in Korea I came back to take up All Saints Church in Bangalore. My own friends did not give me any stationing even after five years. May be God must have spoken to them that Jeevan has to go to some other higher place. I did not have much work. One day Dr. K. C. Abraham, the then Bishop's commissary called me, "why do you waste your time here? There is an offer from NCCI, immediately apply." I sent my application through fax and immediately I got an interview letter. My family members were not willing to send me. I sent another fax saying that my mother was sick and I was not able to attend and hoping that they would select some other person. Rev. Lungmauna, the then General Secretary told me that I was the only candidate. The diocese relieved me for NCCI in 1994.

★ NCCI gave lot of opportunities to National level leadership and visit different places around the world. I had been to Thailand, Philippines, Switzerland, New York, California, Brazil for world mission conference and was a Bible study leader for a group of 20 people around the world and Zimbabwe for WCC assembly and was able to meet great world leaders. I was specially happy to meet the Bishop Lesslie Newbegin who sent me for theological studies.

★ NCCI also gave me an opportunity to spend some time in writing some books. In those five years I spent there, I wrote 12 books published by ISPCK. I was so much privileged that WCC General Secretary released one of those books in Nagpur.

★ While I was there in Nagpur I used to regularly preach at All Saints Cathedral where CNI was formed. Bishop Vinodh Peter used to encourage me so much. He used to sit in the congregation whenever I was preaching. He also gave me an opportunity to be the main Bible study leader by just giving me two days notice for the Nagpur Diocesan Council. I thoroughly enjoyed my ministry in Nagpur.

☆ I had a great experience of going deep in forests of Assam to find a welcome board of my name, and a visit to Mizoram to address the students on their church centenary. I cannot forget the thrilling experience of travelling from Shillong to Mizoram.

☆ I could not come back to the diocese immediately after five years. St. John Church in Fort, Vellore had been in touch with me to take over the church. I asked for the permission from KCD. Since I did not get any response, I thought they do not need me and hence I accepted the call from St. John's Church. I served there for one year where all the CMC doctors and heads of the institutions used to attend. It was a unique church where 96% of the members were from the medical fraternity. One day I happened to meet Bishop Vasanthakumar who had asked me come back to the diocese. I immediately obeyed his order. But before I joined I was asked to meet certain people. They told me that I have to work as fresher with less salary. With tears in my eyes I accepted the challenge because I was committed to Pastoral Ministry. I suffered for one year without proper salary. Nobody realized that my family also suffered due to this. Without any mistake on my side I suffered this punishment. After one year my salary was increased to normal salary. My Church members told me that they will pay me the rest of my salary. I said an emphatic NO. I was happy that I joined my family after six years. I was immediately elected as the convener of the Ministerial committee, which helped me a lot to train young people and to get back into the mainstream of the diocese. Three times I served as the Convener of the Ministerial committee and twice as the Director of Junior Ministers of the Diocese.

☆ I have been suffering from Diabetics since 1983. Which led to kidney problem. It's merely God who was prolonging my ministry and life. When I went to Coimbatore the doctor who checked me told that, "you are a messenger of God,

He has no option except to cure you" I was so glad to listen to such words of encouragement. Bishop Vasanthakumar came home and made arrangement with Manipal Hospital and Dr. Sudharshan Ballal to send the bills of my dialysis to the Diocese for payment, which was a great support and encouraging gesture from the Bishop and the Diocese. I started my dialysis from 17-h September I am doing well now. I hope somebody will donate his or her kidney, I belong to B positive blood group. I need the kidney of B or O blood group person for kidney transplantation. So that I will continue the ministry for some more years, more boldly and creatively than before.

★ In the midst of all these health problems my wife, Kasthuri takes care of me by sacrificing her time as my Dietician, Doctor and 24/7 Nurse. I thank God for her great service to me. My son, Kiran completed his M.S.W. at St. Louis University in US and is now working in New York. I was so glad to see my daughter, Keerthi completing her five-year degree course in B.A. LLB.

★ My journey to Holy land was a great blessing in my life. I never thought that I would step into holy land. But by the grace of God and the interest taken by Bishop Vasanthakumar during my tenure of office as the convener of ministerial committee, all the clergy who completed 25 years of ministry were taken to Holy land. I was one among those privileged. We had a very knowledgeable guide who was a Palestinian Christian, who explained things to us so clearly. We were able to visit Jordan, Israel and Egypt. I felt so privileged to walk where our Lord Jesus walked carrying the cross, where he was transfigured, where he was born, where he performed his miracle in Cana of Galilee, where he raised Lazarus from the tomb, where Jesus was buried, where he was taken to heaven at the last step, Mount Zion and many other related sights of our Lord's ministry. I cannot but simply thank God for the way He led me from a small town of Madanapalle to Jerusalem. A very blessed journey, indeed.

✯ 5th March, 1995 was a very blessed and memorable day for me as I met Mother Teresa in her chamber in Calcutta. For a few minutes as I held her hand, I did not realize where I was. I spent fifteen minutes with her. I thanked God for the great opportunity to meet this great spiritual lady of our century.

My life was a mixture of happy and bad days. I enjoyed the best of all things in every area of my life at every stage of my life. I wish to thank God for the best life he gave me. My father and mother were superb and they gave what ever they could give to me. My mother nurtured me in good discipline. My father gave me lot of encouragement and, moreover it was his dream that I should become a pastor. My brothers and sisters gave me their love and respect. My wife and children were a great source of inspiration for the last 30 years of my life. My father-in-law and my mother-in-law loved me and respected me so much. I am very much indebted to them and to my sisters-in-law and brothers-in-law. I had best teachers in Hope High School, Besant Theosophical College Madanapalle, best teachers in United Theological College, Bangalore. I had a beautiful ministry in all the churches I served. I had the best life in Korea and some good teachers like Dr. Kim Yong Bock and I had the best life in NCCI, Nagpur and every place and country I visited during my NCCI days in spite of being diabetic for the last 25 years. I came from a poor family. We had no popular relatives. But I strongly believe God was journeying with me. When I look back I was at the right place at the right time. I am a little late for St. Matthew's Church. It's a nice Church for me at this age. People are good and programmes of the church are good according to my taste and theology. For all these experiences and God's blessings, should I not thank God? Should you not join with me to say 'thank you God' for me? Indeed God has been good to me throughout the sixty years of my life. I wish to go forward in my life with God as my guide and sustainer and with all your prayers and solidarity through your friendship.

– **Rev. D. S. Jeevan Babu**

2. Photo Album

| S.S.L.C | P.U.C. | B.Com. | M.Th. |

M.Th. Graduation

With Grandmother & Mother

Wedding on 15th May, 1978

Wedding Group Photograph

God Parents Mrs. & Bishop Henry Lazarus

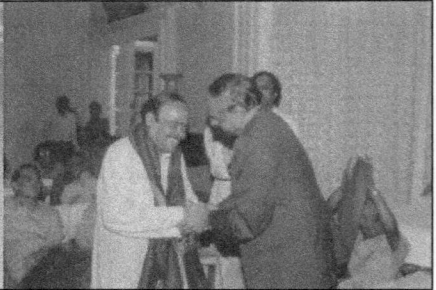

Mr. Rangarajan, Former Governor of A.P. Greeting

Greeting Mr. Devaraj Urs,
Former Chief Minister of Kamataka

At UTC with Arch. Bishop of Canterbury

With former President of Korea

WCC Secretary, Samuel Kada with Hindu
Theological Students, Tirupathi

With Korean Students at Olympic Stadium, Ko   rea

With Indian Ambassador, South Korea

With Rev. Park Chung Chull in Korea   At Tajmahal, Agra

With Orthodox Bishop of Ethiopia   Bible Study Group Leader in Brazil
at Bossey, Switzerland

With former Governor of Karnataka,   With Bishop Leslie Newbigin in Brazil
Mrs. Ramadevi

At Reformation Park in Geneva

At Pyramids in Egypt   At Qumran Caves in Holyland

.... with Family

3. Fullness of Life in Christ for All

The Rt. Rev. Dr. P. Surya Prakash*

What is Life?

Each of you would give different answers.

For some, it is a pleasant thing but for others, it is a burden. For some, it is a bed of roses but for others, it is a bed of thorns. Our answers vary depending upon who we are and in which state of life we are in.

There are different aspects of life:

Individual life, Collective life, or Group life, Community life, Life of a nation etc. Social life, dealing with inter-actions and relations; Cultural life, dealing with aspects aesthetic value; Religious life/spiritual life/church life, dealing with things of mind, soul or spirit.

Categories:

> Modern life,
> Traditional life,
> City life or urban life,
> Village life or life in the rural contexts.

Life is something that has to do with living beings, animals, birds and people.

TV Serial: Animal Life, National Geographic Channel, Discovery channel etc.

Rt. Rev Dr. Surya Prakash who is currently serving as a Bishop of Karinmnagar Diocese, was a classmate of Rev. Jeevan Babu at UTC.

Life is something creative, dynamic and lively over against death and decay.

Life has a beginning and an end (Christ is Alpha and Omega). See Genesis 1.1, Rev.21.1.

Life is considered as a journey. Life sets us in motion.

Life is measurable: days, weeks, months and years (Age of life – Infant, child, youth, adolescent, adult, middle-aged, old etc). See Ps.90.12

Life has the length of time (2004) and the point of time (12.01.04), See Ps.118

Life also has a time span: past, present and future (yesterday, today, and tomorrow).

According to Hindu samsara, life is an endless cycle of births and deaths. Life goes on in circles.

Life has basic needs: like food, shelter, clothing (roti, kapda aur Makaan).

Life consists of Body.

Life has aesthetic needs. Life consists of mind.

Life has emotional needs. Life consists of feelings.

Life has spiritual needs. Life has a spirit (athma and longs for paramathma).

St. Augustine's famous observation: Our souls are restless until they find their rest in you.

Meaning of life is to be found in God.

"Human beings shall not live by bread alone but by every word that comes out of the mouth of the Lord." Deuteronomy 8.3

"Where could we go, you have the words of eternal life."
John 6.68

Jesus calls upon his followers:

Love the Lord your God, with all your heart, with all your
mind, with all your strength, with all your soul.

Life has many aspects and it is important. Therefore respect
to life and protection of life and sustainability of life are very
crucial: Civil society has developed the concept of

> Human Rights,
>
> Fundamental Rights,
>
> Civil Rights,
>
> Minority Rights etc.
>
> These rights speak of values in life: right to life, right
> to work, right to privacy, right to speak, right to move
> and right to freedom of speech etc.

Life has many dimensions and it is a complex phenomenon.

What is Fullness of Life?

Life in all its fullness, completeness, wholeness, perfection,
totality etc

Life in which all the needs – physical, mental/ intellectual,
ethical/ moral, spiritual/religious, emotional, aesthetic, social
are met.

Opposite of fullness is emptiness. One time or the other
we will all experience emptiness especially when we have no
work to do, specially for those who have retired from active
service. All those who have retired can opt for volunteer service
undertaken in the community where they live. There is enough
volunteer work in India. Life can become self-centred and
major concern might be one's own peace and comfort. I am
reminded of the words of Fosdick's hymn: God of grace and

God of glory:

> Shame our wanton, selfish gladness,
> Rich in things and poor in soul,
> Grant us wisdom, grant us courage,
> Lest we miss thy kingdom's goal.

Busyness is not the answer, then neither is the emptiness. Living one's own life leaves life empty. A search must continue for God's will, for some mission, for some kingdom goal that will bring meaning to life.

Fullness cannot be achieved if we have not felt true feeling of emptiness.

We need to recognise that there are limitations of life. Paul is the greatest example of it. He wrote: I have learned, in whatever state I am, to be content" Phil.4.11. This does not mean that he has become complacent or unconcerned. He means that he could be independent of circumstances, that nothing could shake his inner strength, peace in Christ. Life in Christ.

One day, a person was asked what he wants or wishes in his life? He answered: I desire from life, health, love, beauty, fame, and fortune." The old man told him: you missed the most important thing: What is that, he asked: Peace of mind, replied the old man.

What is Fullness of Life in Christ?

John 10:10: "I have come that you might have life and have it abundantly."

What is he talking about?

1 John 5:12: "Whoever has the son has life, whoever does not have the Son of God, does not have life.

John 3:36: "Whoever believes in the Son has eternal life; whoever disobeys the Son will not see life, but must endure God's wrath."

"In him was life, the life was light of all people." John 1.4

Jesus' affirmations in the Gospel of John :

4.14; 7.37 (Jesus is the water of life)

6.35   I am the bread of life

8.12   I am the light of the world

1:11   I am the good shepherd

11.25   I am the resurrection and the life

14.6   I am the way, and the truth and the life

15.1   I am the true vine

Truly, a very extra-ordinary life. Jesus has something new to offer.

John's Gospel is the Gospel of life. Fullness in Christ. John 1.16, Col 1.19, 2.9

Wholeness means our inner peace is not taken by the events of life. Troubles, distresses, and anxieties cannot be set aside, but God's grace can be counted upon to deliver us through the trials and temptations. That is fullness of life.

What is Fullness of Life in Christ for All?

See John 3.16: ... that whosoever believes on him should not perish but have life.

Mathew11.28: Come unto me all that labour and are heavy laden, I will give you rest.

Gen. 2.3: "In you, all the families of the earth shall be blessed."

Amos 9.7: "God is the liberator of all oppressed people" (Luke 4.19-21).

Mathew 5.45: The blessings of nature are for all. God makes his sun rise on the evil and on the good, and sends rain on the righteous and the unrighteous."

Acts 17.27: "God is not far from any one."

2 Peter 3.9:"God does not want anyone to perish."

There is no discrimination. God's love is for all.

Fullness of God: Eph.3.19, 4.13, Col 2.9

The Church being the Body of Christ has a special role in life. It is called upon to fulfil the work of Christ.

Fullness or Wholeness of Life: Vision & Reality

Isaiah 65.17-25: The vision of a glorious new creation.

Luke 7.11-35: The reality of a new creation.

Rev. 21.1-4 (22.1-5): New heaven and new earth.

Our context is a modern society, which is characterised by consumerism, travel, building etc.

It is a progressive society in many ways. One word that characterises it is globalisation.

We are in a globalised world with instant communication, fast travel and fast transportation of goods and ideas, images and pictures.

In this world there is good and bad, health and sickness, affluence and poverty, beauty and ugliness and above all a few enjoy the life while many are deprived and suffer. Not only the poor who suffer but even the nature suffers with all its flora and fauna. Dalits in our country have been suffering for ages.

But God has a different plan and purpose for this world. The prophets have seen it and Jesus has implemented it.

One of the greatest of the prophets of the Hebrew nation was Isaiah. As it is recorded in 65th chapter he sees a vision of glorious new creation in the context of exile, when everything was lost.

New heavens and new earth,

Jerusalem as a joy and its people as a delight;

No more sound of weeping or cry of distress;

No infant mortality but there shall be long life,

People shall build houses and inhabit them,

Plant vineyards and eat their fruit.

They shall enjoy the work of their hands.

They shall not labour in vain and they shall be blessed by God.

Their prayers shall be heard.

Above all, there will be harmony in nature, peace and integrity in creation. See v.25.

It is no more the survival of the fittest only but the weak and the strong together. Every valley shall be filled and every mountain shall be brought low.

What a dream? What a vision? What more can we dream of? What more can we ask for?

Our emphasis today at this hour is that church is a community of liberation.

God has given fullness of life.

God wants us to be partakers of this fullness of life.

God wants us to be sharers of this fullness of life.

(Cloth has been made use of as a symbol. Cloth stands for covering oneself, for protecting oneself and also for image and beauty).

But the question is, liberation from what to what?

What is the reality in India?

People who live in the slums are the highest in the world.

Infant mortality, the highest,

Malnutrition of children, the highest,

Child abuse, the highest,

Child labour, the highest,

Oppression and exploitation of women, the highest,

Discrimination based on caste, creed or colour, region, language, the highest.

Those who have every means of livelihood, security, and enjoyment say, it is blessed to be born in India. But those who do not, say, it is a curse to be born in India.

An economist has said: to be born poor is to die early, and to be born rich is to live long.

How true!

If the church is also a reflection of the society, woe unto it.

At the time of Jesus, as we see from the gospel narratives, it was a sick society. Something similar to ours.

We have a society of commerce without ethics,

of pleasure without conscience,

of politics without principles,

of knowledge without character,

of science without humanity,

of wealth without work,

and of worship without sacrifice.

We have tall buildings but short tempers,

We have bigger houses but shorter families.

We have higher incomes but lower morals.

We have more food but lesser appetite

We have more acquaintances but few friends,

We have more information but less communication.

We have more conveniences but less time,

We have more knowledge but less judgement,

We have more degrees but less commonsense.

We have more experts but more problems.

We have more medicine but less health.

We have multiplied our possessions but reduced our values.

We talk too much but listen too little.

We have learnt how to make a living but not life.

We have added years to life and not life to years.

We laugh too little,

We drive too fast,

We get too angry too quickly,

We stay up too late and get up too tired.

We read too seldom and watch TV too much

And we pray too seldom.

Is this our life? This is the paradox of our time.

At the time of Jesus there was so much of blindness, deafness, lameness, leprosy and death. All Jesus' energy seems to have been spent on healing the people and casting out demons.

We read in Luke the reality is being changed.

And the news of this new reality is spread all over like a wild fire. The news reach even prison walls and rooms.

John the Baptist's spirit was lifted up. His eyes are filled with new hope and expectations and he asks:

Are you the one or are we to wait for another? He is eager to know. Time is running out.

Jesus does not reply directly. Instead, he tells him to report what they have seen and heard.

What did they see? What did they hear? It is gospel in action what they see and hear.

The blind receive their sight,

The lame walk,

The lepers are cleansed,

The deaf hear,

The dead are raised,

And the poor have good news brought to them.

That is the fullness of life in Christ. That's the new heaven and the new earth, here and now.

Supposing, we were asked to provide evidence that our church really is bringing good news to the poor and to the community. What activities would you list as your credentials? There is a popular song: "Don't just talk about love. Show me." How much has your church done to make access easy for the poor and the disabled? What concern have you shown for the poor? How welcome is the stranger? These are our witnesses to the reality of the gospel.

The purpose of the human existence is life. The very first blessing of God is: Be fruitful and multiply ... Genesis 1.28. The Church is called to propagate the good news of life in fullness in the world where the powers of death are at work. In a world where injustice, suppression, hunger and other powers of death prevail, the propagation of life in fullness demands a uncompromising attitude in the service of justice and for the total liberating of humanity in the name of Jesus. "You are to name him Jesus, for he shall liberate his people from their sins." Matthew 1.21.

From the biblical point of view, the abundance of good things is an invitation to enjoy life. It is necessary to struggle for a better life for all, but the joy of life and the celebration of life is more important. A philosopher of life in OT says: I know that there is nothing better for them than to be happy and enjoy themselves as long as they live; It is God's gift that all should eat and drink and take pleasure in their toil" Ecclesiastes 3.12-13.

It is one of the clichés in the west about the Third World that people are often happy and celebrating their life if situations allow them to do so. Indeed, many poor people in Africa, Asia and Latin America do not let the joy of life and the enjoyment of all things be taken away from them. This joy belongs to their life and it helps them to overcome time, which seem to be hopeless.

In the west the wheel has turned a full circle. After experiencing great economic progress and reaching a stage of saturation, some of the people are now asking:

Do we have an affluent society or life in fullness?

People are gradually recognising that life does not consist of things one possesses. Luke 12.15: But life is more than things.

There is so much invisible suffering inside the doors – loneliness, sickness, depression, meaningless. In spite of best food and nutrition and care and fitness centres, regular exercises and free time and vacations, the clinics are full with sick people. To get an appointment with a specialist you need weeks.

Of course, the biblical understanding of a life in fullness has also, and even especially, consequences for the industrialised countries. Here, the difference between an affluent society and a life in fullness has to be recognised, and consequences have to be drawn.

Despite of the affluent offers of consumer goods many people are aware that this is no life in fullness and that the signs of crisis in the society are threatening the future. The impoverishment of large groups of the population, the growing gap between the financial problems of the State and the enormous profits of big firms, the increasing crime rate, the manifold threats to the environment, the fears of many children and adults regarding their future. Alternatives are needed, and the biblical concept of a life in fullness can be a good starting point.

People are on the search for meaning in life. A great deal of Buddhist meditation and yoga centres are on the increase in Europe. Some people are fed up with materialism and asking for new ways of finding meaning in life. Unfortunately, we are following the western model of development. We are on the way also for a great disappointment. Bread for the World and Development Agencies are asking whether 50 years of development aid really eradicated poverty and made people self-reliant or made them dependent? The modern development concept inherited from the west coupled with globalisation has already killed the livelihood of millions in the third world.

In the church, commitment for development of the biblical concept of a life in fullness can give many suggestions and can serve as a means for orientation. At first, it is necessary to become aware of this fullness, i.e., the fullness of natural resources and human abilities and knowledge. To this, the question adds how this richness can be used and conserved for the good of human beings as well as for the good of the whole creation.

The community life belongs also to a life in fullness. Therefore, a village community can have a high value in a developmental commitment. At the same time, it is necessary to counteract everything, which obstructs a life in fullness.

A great challenge in India for us to counteract the commercialisation of life by the media. Life is glorified by the film world and the order of the society seems to be the survival of the fittest.

When Cardinal Paulo Evaristo Arns laid down his office as Archbishop of Sao Paulo in 1996 when he was 75 years old, he stated once again what a life in fullness means: "We Christians believe in the human being and in the human person as criterions of all systems and economic systems. Technology and development have to serve the poor. ...We face one of the biggest challenges in human history: to share possession and knowledge with all and attempt to save our planet from greedy robbers who pounce upon the wood, life and precious things and who cause the ecological tragedy of soil and our global environment. The propagation of life, of life in fullness, must remain the horizon of our work.

Development with a human face.

The verses from the 23rd Psalm give comfort and hope for a life in fullness to many millions of people:

The Lord is my shepherd, I shall not want. He makes me lie down in green pastures; He leads me beside still waters; he restores my soul. He leads me in right paths for his name's sake. (Ps. 23, 1-3)

A girl once recited this Psalm and said: The Lord is my shepherd. That's all I want.

Fullness or wholeness of life:

Fullness of life not only for human beings, but also for all creation.

Where do we go from here? What do we need to do?

First, let us accept life as a gift of God. And let us handle it with care.

Second, let us make life a blessing for us and for others. Life consists of relationships.

Let us live and make others live. See Micah 6.8.

Third, let us accept the Beatitudes (Mathew 5.1-10) as principles of life:

Four, let us make the Fruit of the Spirit (Galatians 5.22-23) our attitude in life.

4. In Fullness of Life: Role of Law and Judiciary

*Mrs. Porkodi Prabhakaran**

Jesus said as in St. John 10:10, " I have come that they may have life and have it in full." In God was life and the life was the light of men (John 1:4). This light should shine before all the people that they may see our good deeds and praise our Father in Heaven. So the wholeness of life depends on the voltage of the light, which makes our good deeds visible, and in turn our Father in Heaven is praised. God, the WORD, became flesh and made His dwelling among us with fullness of grace and truth. When we give our life to this CHRIST we get the gift of 'fullness of life'. God has not given us the spirit of fear but of power (to live constructively) and of love (to live sacrificially) and of a sound mind (to live reasonably). God has given us a spiritual manual of operations, so that we enjoy the fullness of life. As we read in John 10:9, Christ is the gate and we the sheep enter through this gate, come in and go out and find pasture. Coming in i.e., going into the fold means to find security, which we all deeply desire in this troubled and anxious world. If we enter through Jesus Christ we do not have to worry about the nuclear threat or the crime rate or the zigs and zags of an uncertain economy. Jesus is our security and is incharge of all things. Going our means to find liberty – liberty to move into life in any dimension. Christ should come into our hearts so that we shall have an abundant life – a life filled with excitement and adventure.

Mrs. Porkodi Prabhakaran, Principal of Bishop Cotton Women Christian Law College where Rev. Jeevan Babu served as the Vice Chairman of the board of management.

In fullness of life, the law and judiciary do play a role. In the light of the above said prologue, we could say that the ingredients of ' fullness of life' are:

❖ Constructive, sacrificial and reasonable living;

❖ Living with security and moving out with liberty;

❖ Living a life of excitement and adventure;

The origin of law was from Mount Sinai. From this Mosaic sprouted out the Roman jurisprudence, which was the basis for the common law of England from which enactment of Indian laws was made. *How far the enacted laws contribute for a constructive and reasonable living? And do we get the security in life and the liberty to move out to do adventurous acts with all excitement?* The answer to these questions will highlight the role of law and judiciary in fullness of life.

The supreme vital document of democratic India is the Constitution. The preamble to the Constitution says,

> "We the people of India having solemnly resolved to constitute India into a sovereign, socialist, democratic, secular republic and secure to all its citizens.
>
> Justice, social, economic, and political
>
> Liberty, of thought, expression, belief, faith and worship;
>
> Equality, of status and of opportunity;
>
> And to promote among them all fraternity assuring the dignity of the individual and the unity and the integrity of the nation."

The whole preamble brings out the entire ingredients of the fullness of life. Articles 12 to 34 of the Constitution enumerate the fundamental rights. Equality before law (Art 14) is the breath that gives life to various legislations balancing the rights of the citizens. The weaker sections of the society and the downtrodden are protected and their status is elevated by giving preferential rights / reservations in the legislator – elections, in appointments and promotions etc. God makes the sun to rise on the evil and the good and sends rain on the just and on the unjust. The traditicnal culture, having been the cloaks for denying the rights to women has been torn down to bestow equal rights irrespective of gender. Many legislations for the welfare of the women are in force now. All their rights are guaranteed under these statutes. Hindu women are now given rights on par with their male counterparts in ancestral properties too as per the amendment made in the Hindu Succession Act, Dowry Prohibition Act 1961, Protection of Women from Domestic Violence Act 2005, The Indecent Representation of Women (prohibition) Act 1986, The Immoral Traffic (prevention) Act, 1956 and such statutes bestow rights on Women which become protective cloak to them and also to get to the fore on par with men. Provisions have been made in the Indian Penal Code, Criminal Procedure Code and the Indian Evidence Act by way of amendments to protect women from cruelty, harassment and other offences and social evils (For instance, section 304B IPC- for eradiation of the social evil of dowry which is the bane of Indian society; section 498 A, section 113 of the Indian Evidence Act and section 357 of criminal procedure code are similar instances). Conjugal rights are recognised in matrimonial laws depending on the religion they profess.

Laws recognising the rights of children are in force. Children's rights are protected under the Child Marriage Restraint Act 1929, Prevention of Child Labour Act and so many other Acts and rules. Guidelines are there for adoption of children both from inland and foreign apart from the Hindu Adoption and Maintenance Act. Right to education is made a fundamental right to childhood and right to food, shelter and maintenance. But it is alarming to note that injustice is meted our to girl children. Female infanticide and foeticide are on the increase. No specific law is in force to prevent these two evils. Parental Diagnostic Technologies Act (PNDT Act) is sufficient to address these evils.

Senior citizens are given many privileges. But no specific law has been enacted except the provision as found in section 125 of Criminal Procedure Code. But judgments are there to protect and maintain parents even by the daughters. Consumers are protected well under Consumer Protection Act.

Terrorism is on its peak. Legislations like Prevention of Terrorist Activities Act help in no way. Everyone feels insecure. The recent terrorist attack in Mumbai speaks volumes. Women are not secured to move around.

Religious intolerance, regionalism, language fanaticism and so on have made the wall of security crumble down. The beauty and pride of our county is that it is a secular state. A secular state has no religion of its own. A secular county treats all regions equally. Articles 25 to 28 of the constitution give concrete shape to the concept of secularism. It guarantees to every person the freedom of conscience and the right to profess, practice and propagate religion. Article 30 confers a right on the religious linguistic minorities because of their numerical handicap and to instil in them a sense of security and confidence. But the security, today, of the minorities is at stake. In Orissa and Karnataka churches have been attacked; nuns have been sexually harassed; worship services have to go on with police security.

The essence of secularism in India is the recognition and preservation of the different types of people with diverse language and different beliefs and placing them together. In spite of all the protection given to the minorities under the constitution there is an ongoing violence and injustice against the minorities. But the recent judgment sentencing death and life imprisonment to the attacker of church makes us take our hats off to the judiciary. Regionalism has led to terrorism and violence. We as a so-called civilised society, share a huge burden of guilt in this escalation of violence in spite of various legislation and contributions by the judiciary. Thus laws are enacted for giving security to people but effectiveness of such laws is not worth mentioning. "Written laws are like spider's webs; they will catch, it is true, the weak and the poor; but would be torn in pieces by the rich and powerful" – Anonymous. This is our sad plight.

LIBERTY is enjoyed by few and for the majority it is a mirage. The prevailing condition in the country seems to negate the right of liberty. No more words are needed to explain in detail.

Judiciary or judicial system is the system of courts, which administer justice. The law holds together the fabric of the nation. The concept of social justice is the yardstick to the justice administration system or the legal justice and it would be an obligation for the law courts to apply the law depending upon the situation in a manner whichever is beneficial to the society. Social justice is the device to ensure life to be meaningful and livable with human dignity. The medium of social justice is an umbrella term to deliver justice. The role of judiciary is to interpret laws and administer justice. Legal services authority render service to the society by giving legal aid to the poor and needy, women and children, the weak and the downtrodden, the oppressed and the exploited etc. Human rights are recognised and National and State Human Rights Commission come to the rescue of the victims of inhuman acts.

The virus of corruption has intruded into the judiciary and the balance of justice is titled towards the affluent. Reasonable living with dignity and honour, which the constitution guarantees to have fullness of life, stays afar. The Lokayukta of Karnataka State ventures much to use the scalpel of punishment to get rid of the virus of corruption. Political interference has some-time bent the rod of justice. Lord Bowen says "Justice is like a blind man in a dark room looking for a black cat which is not here." It is very much unfortunate,

---

'I am happy that the children of Rev. D.S. Jeevan Babu have taken this initiative to publish a volume to commemorate the 60th year of their father. I congratulate them and wish Jeevan Babu many more years of ministry in the Church.'

"Injustice anywhere is a threat to justice everywhere"- said Martin Luther. The Chief Justice of India has recommended that any judicial officer who is unfit, ineffective, incompetent or has doubtful integrity may be retired from service. The Minister of Law and Justice, H.R. Bharadwaj has informed the Lok Sabha, in a letter dated 14th October, 2008 that the Chief Justice of India has said that if implemented in rights earnest, such a provision will keep deviant behaviour in check besides getting rid of those who are found to be indolent, ineffective or with doubtful integrity (vide The New Indian Express dated 13th December, 2008, page 07).

This seems to be a silver lining in the dark clouds of deteriorating integrity in the judiciary.

Ways are paved for concrete, sacrificial and reasonable living by the law and the judiciary, with obstacles of course, affording fullness of life. Many legislations guarantee such concrete, sacrificial and reasonable living with dignity. But their effectiveness is little as the people do not make use of such statutes in their fullest measure due to various reasons like ignorance and indifference.

Security and liberty are guaranteed in the Preamble of the Constitution and enshrined as Fundamental Rights, which give fullness of life. But the law and the judiciary, though have not played absolute role in protecting the most vulnerable and innocent members of our society, have indeed extended their arms to offer means for security and liberty. The people should reach our to get the benefit of the extended arm. Braving this sort of storm of 'insecurity' and 'no liberty', we have to make the people aware of all the laws through which various rights are offered – the laws which do not have a role in fullness of life. Judiciary should be above all kinds of influence and pressures. The global issue of economic meltdown, which has caused a serious crisis, should be addressed adventurously for which the law and the judiciary should play their role effectively to safeguard our country from being infected with such crisis.

To conclude, it can be said that the fullness of life could be secured only when we are in Christ and we get fullness of joy in His presence as we inherit the Christ like qualities to honour God and the State. We get the security, liberty, justice and peace when Christ rules in our hearts, which are exposed and exercised through the law and the judiciary.

I take this opportunity to wish Rev. Jeevan Babu on completing 60 years of age to have a long, healthy, happy and blessed life, of course, in its fullness and I thank him for giving me this opportunity.

5. Theological Reflection: Life in all its Fullness

Rev. Dr. K.C. Abraham*

The Editor of this volume has asked me to reflect on the general theme 'Life in all its Fullness' with a special emphasis on the role of Christian theology. Theology is not an abstract science; it is about life, abundant life. We celebrate this life and live this life. Theological reflection is a second act.

The starting point for our theological reflection on life is the affirmation that life is God's gift. It has not sprung from nothing accidentally. It is created by God for a purpose. The fundamental value of creation is derived from the fact that it is created.

Diversity is the hallmark of creation. All humans and non-human creatures animate and inanimate things, air and space, light and darkness together make up our created order. Unity in Diversity is possible when all the different elements work together for the common good. God has not created the creatures as a homogenous entity. They all do not look alike – the sameness and uniformity is not God's purpose. In fact in the globalised monoculture we tend to suppress diversity – for it is either inconvenient or not profitable. Diversity has to be preserved. Diversity in shape, colour, size and other aspects of appearances add to the beauty of creation.

Not all are endowed with the same talents and gifts. Unfortunately, we tend to regard human beings and others

---

*Rev. Dr. K.C. Abraham, a renowned theologian, who was instrumental in sending Rev. Jeevan Babu to NCCI.

according to their use-value. For this reason we do not consider those who are born with disabilities as equal to the able-bodied. Their disabilities apart, they have been excluded from society by prejudice and stigma. The worth of an individual is not decided by their usefulness or the status of their birth or social position. But based on the fact they are created by God. Intrinsic value of a person is the basis of an equal society. We believe God is concerned about the weak, powerless and disabled not because of their merits, but because they happen to be His children. Let us celebrate every life, even the smallest and the weakest.

Life is sustained and enhanced by a set of relationships. This relational understanding of human nature has given a new perspective for life. In the ancient world, under the influence of Greek philosophy we were used to substantiality categories of thought. What is the essence or substance of human and things? This seems to be the predominant question.

Soul/body dualism became the basis of our reflection. But relational understanding has rejected this dualism and constructed a discourse based on relationships. The essence of human nature does not consist of an irreducible principle or substances, but in a fulfilling and meaningful relationship. God's nature is experienced as relationship of love or awe. Our addressability to God is the expression of our image of God in us. For this reason relationship between humans assume a special significance. In fact our theological and ethical reflection has to be directed towards enhancing the tenuous relationship that forge between human beings. Relationships are sustained by values and structures. The values like love, justice and concern for the other are rooted in our vision of God's kingly rule (Basielia). Our Lord has given an invaluable insight into the work of structures in the famous words "Sabbath is not for human but human for Sabbath." Sabbath stands of the tradition, law and institutional structures. They should serve human. The problem of structural fundamentalism is to be abhorred.

Life is God's precious gift; it has to be preserved and enhanced. This seems to be a universal truth acknowledged by all faiths and ideologies. However, Moses at this farewell speech brings a concrete dimension to this universal vision: Life is God's gift –nevertheless it is enhanced by our choices and decisions. There are life affirming forces as well as death dealing systems and traditions. In this situation, our responsibility to keep life by our choices becomes urgent. "I call heaven and earth to witness against you today that I have set before you life and death, blessings and curses. Choose life so that you and your descendants may live, loving the Lord your God, obeying him, and holding fast to him; for that means life to you and length of days, so that you may live in the land that the Lord swore to give to your ancestors, to Abraham, to Isaac, and to Jacob (Deut. 30:19 & 20). How do we choose life? Moses commands, 'by loving the Lord your God, walking in his ways, and observing his commandments, decrees and ordinances'. They are not mere legal codes. They are instituted for preserving life and its relationships. Our Lord has given the summary of the Ten Commandments 'love God with all your heart, mind and soul and love your neighbour as yourself.' Living sensitively to God and to others – fellow human beings and God's creation – life finds its fulfilment.

To believe in the God of life is to affirm the supremacy of life over death. This means, "any assault on life –hunger, destitution, squalor, oppression and injustice- is an attack on God" (Gutierrez).

In the light of this we can look at our situation where life is being threatened, vitiated and destroyed. Our wilful resistance to God's demand to choose life, and our refusal to participate in God's life- giving activity are expressed in many ways. From dowry deaths to nuclear disasters one can draw a list of violent acts we commit to one another and to nature. Our faith in the God of life has to be expressed as values, practices and institutions that affirm and enhance life, and as denouncement of systems and structures that diminish and extinguish the lives of so many.

Jesus' life and mission is understood as life giving. He was the messiah. Many people in his time, however, considered the messiah as the crusading Raja who would demolish the Roman Empire. But his peace loving approach to life was met with doubt by his own cousin, John the Baptist. He grew suspicious of the intentions of Jesus. He sent emissaries to ask whether he was really the messiah (Mt.11:1).

Jesus told them to see what he was doing. "The blind receive sight, the lame walk, the lepers are cleansed, the deaf hear, the dead are raised and the poor have good news brought to them." This succinctly expresses the messianic style of life giving. Healing, wholeness, solidarity with the suffering, hope for the hopeless – these are some of the dimensions of it. Jesus proclaimed 'life' standing along with those who are victimized, dispossessed and marginalised. "Where Jesus is, there is life: there is abundant life, rigorous life, loved life and eternal life (Moltmann). The process of life giving is to bring dignity, justice and wholeness to those who are extinguished.

Jesus' uncompromising defense of life led him to a life of conflict with the powerful ruling class of his time. This conflict led him to his death. But the Resurrection is the affirmation that God's last words was not death but life. Jesus' witness to life in its fullness has these two sides to it: solidarity with the oppressed and conflict with the oppressor.

Some Implications

A Reversal of Capitalist Logic of Accumulation

To have and possess more seems to be the goal of most people in life. The logic of the growth oriented, capitalist economy is accumulation and profit. Jesus in these verses gives counter logic of growth. Giving and losing seems to be the way of saving life. Jesus himself showed it in his own life. His life is expended for others. Love is not hedonistic pleasure, and happiness does not depend on consumerism. It is costly and self-giving. The other, the stranger and the poor take on a priority for us. This requires hard choices and an unpopular life style. In this sense a Christian is the odd man/woman out there.

Certainly, most of us cannot be Mother Teresa, completely selfless. But all of us can be in our day-to-day life, be more considerate about the needs and problems of the have-nots. We can also work towards a system of economic life that works with a logic counter to that of capitalism. In a study of globalisation by the UN in 2000 it was observed that notwithstanding the benefits of the process, there is skewing of care services. Our system is not designed to care for the weak and the marginal.

Our churches and institutions are engaged in development schemes; we need resources for our programmes and we cannot anymore be dependant on external funding. But in our eagerness to develop our land and other resources, we too are being co-opted by the logic of capitalism. Seldom do we get a chance to even raise a critical voice to the capitalist values that are entrenched in our economic practices. In this situation, how do we witness to life in its fullness?

Life in its Fullness: Feeding the Hungry

Jesus' use of bread as a symbol of life is important. Here a generic (root) vision of life takes on a concrete dimension. So for Jesus, feeding the hungry is part of the life-giving mission of God. He taught them many things and he fed them. Both acts are inseparable.

The command "You give them something to eat" has a contemporary ring to it. In a recent report of the UN it is said that India is the home of the largest number of the world's hungry. But the irony is that we claim to have attained self-sufficiency in food. Our storehouses have food grains sufficient enough to feed all the people. Why do people have to go hungry? There is something wrong, somewhere.

Our Lord told the disciples, "You give them something to eat." They naturally thought of money to buy food. We too think about development projects, external funding etc., to take care of the hungry. All these may be necessary. But Jesus seems to indicate that the prerequisite to feeding the hungry is 'sharing'. The miracle is in the act of sharing – quite contrary to our tendency to hoard and accumulate. It was an enactment of the central message of our Lord: the broken God for a broken people. The bread had to be broken and shared. Apostle Paul was quite clear that the Lord's Supper was administered only after all of them had eaten together. We need a sharing attitude, but more important, policies and structures that ensure an even distribution of basic resources.

Life in its Fullness: Eternal Life

He was young, prosperous and religious. He could be in modern times the executive of an IT company. But he was restless. In this confused world of conflicts and contradictions, how do you make any sense? Developing this thought would have driven him to Jesus with the question, "What must I do to inherit eternal life?" This question represents a desire to get away from this world and to be secure in the comfort zone of spiritual bliss. Eternal life is often perceived as life beyond. But Jesus brings him back to the nitty gritty. He starts with making an appeal to moral life. This had no impact on him, as he was so sure of his moral achievements. Then comes the punch line. "Give away all what you have to the poor." A difficult, almost an impossible command to follow. But that is the point. Eternal life is not merely an extension of the virtuous and self-righteous life of his, but comes as a result of drastic and fundamental change – a metanoia.

Here we may recall the story of another young man in Luke 15. He too was from an affluent background and grew restless. His search for a meaning in life, eternal life, took him to a far-away land and a life that isolated himself from his home, seeking pleasures for himself. Disillusioned, he returns home and finds a new meaning in the unconditional acceptance of him by his father. That is metanoia, a turning around, the only condition for entering into eternal life.

How concretely do you experience eternal life? Not as life after death or as longevity of years of life; but by responding to the challenges of the other – the marginal and the poor. The young man came to Jesus seeking eternal life, but Jesus confronted him with a demand:

> "sell all what you have and give to the poor." Only in solidarity with the struggles of the poor can we experience the eternal here and now.

Life in its Fullness: New Creation

We are committed to a vision of human wholeness, which includes not only our relationship with one another, but also our relationship vis-à-vis nature and the universe.

In the New Testament, Christ's work of redemption extends to the whole universe. Christ, the Lord of history, initiates a process of transformation that moves towards cosmic release (Eph.1:1-10; and Col. 1: 15-20). The unity between the hope for inward liberation of the children of God and the liberation of the entire physical creation from its bondage and oppression is the theme of Rom.8. Ktisis, translated as 'creation' means not only women and men, but all created things including demonic powers. It is in the search for liberation of all aspects of human life and all created life and natural environment that we can truly affirm salvation, in the wholeness of creation.

Thanks to the many environmental movements in Europe, USA and other parts of the world, there is a greater awareness of the ecological crisis. There is, however, a relative indifference to the wider questions of justice when we discuss this issue.

The inter-connectedness of the renewal of society and the renewal of the earth is clearly seen in all the struggles of the marginalised – indigenous groups, dalits, fishermen and landless poor. The profit-oriented growth destroys the eco-balance as well as the poor: their villages, their forests and their people. Let the cry of the poor and the groaning of creation be the focal point of our faith and spirituality.

Life in its Fullness: Crossing Cultural/Religious Boundaries

The Christian Church was begun as an exclusive community – a Jewish sect. A section within the early Christian Church, known as the Judaistic party, even insisted that all those who became Christians should accept all religious/communal rites of Judaism. Peter being proud of his Jewishness was sympathetic to this but the spirit breaks him out of this isolation – breaks him out of the box he put himself. Acts.10 describes this in detail and a report of this is given in Acts.11: 1-18

We see the picture of Peter in a box. The box is formed by cultural, ethnic or religious heritage. Many of us like Peter prefer to remain in the security and comfort of the boxes created by ethnicity. Like Peter, seldom are we aware of being in a box. What is important, however, is that Peter broke out of it. The spirit provides a vision of reality that goes beyond the narrow confines. In our social life we are beleaguered by casteism, communalism and regionalism that divide life. Unfortunately, we as Christians and our claims for exclusiveness and superiority contribute to such divisive forces. Life in its fullness has to be experienced as crossing those boundaries.

"To reject exclusivism and to accept plurality, to be committed to one's faith and to be open to the faith commitments of our neighbour's, to choose to live in a global community of communities, sharing the ambiguities of history and the mystery of life - these are the imperatives of life" (Samartha).

6. Role of Christian Values

*Dr. Moses P. Manohar**

Dear Kiran and Keerthi,

I am happy to write this note on Christian values as you celebrate 60 years of life and ministries of your father and my friend and colleague Rev. D.S. Jeevan Babu. I am particularly happy that both of you have grown up and have become professionals. I appreciate your efforts to prepare a festschrift as part of the celebration. I record my hearty greetings to your parents Rev. Jeevan Babu and Mrs. Jeevan Babu for a long life and ministry. It brings to my mind a lot of pleasant memories of our days in the National Council of Churches in India (NCCI). However, I would like to concentrate on the topic you have assigned for my reflection.

Values

Human beings are known as moral beings. We have moral codes and principles as our guides for our life. Therefore we have "OK" and "not OK" behaviour in our day-to-day living. Values are considered as the most estimable things in life. Religions can be described as the fountainheads of values. Jesus and his early followers were pioneers in setting new values for human beings. Those Christian values were instrumental to human emancipation universally. Let me share a few of them.

Dr. Moses P. Manohar, serving as the Director of ICSA was a friend and colleague, Secretary at NCCI, Nagpur.

1. Forgiving the Enemies

Avenging the enemy is considered as a heroic action. Even in our Indian films both the villain and the hero prove their supremacy over the other by destroying and annihilating the enemies. But when Jesus prayed for forgiveness of his tormenters while hanging on the cross, he exhibited a value of forgiving the enemies. Jesus taught us not to take revenge against the enemies but forgive them and pray for them. Forgiveness transforms a society of mutual enemies into a society of friends. Throughout the Christian era, thousands of men and women who suffered injustice and pain openly forgave their perpetrators and went on praying for them. When Mrs. Graham Stains openly announced that she forgave those who killed her husband and two minor sons gruesomely, she enacted this Christian value of forgiving enemies. History has proved that forgiving the enemy is more powerful to change the people rather than punishing them.

2. Equality

Equality of all human beings is a great value. Christianity was a pioneer to make this as a fundamental guide for Christian living. In the early Christian era, the idea of the church as that it is a body, which recognises not inequality and difference among its members. In the ancient period, people had to prove their identity for their safety and survival. People were secure when they were among those who share the same cultural identity, which included the eating habit, dress code, special occupation, religious ceremonies and rituals etc. By observing these exclusive practices, people asserted their identity. Therefore, exclusion was the primary code for identity among various kinds of people. But when Christians were drawn from Jewish, Greek, Roman, Arabic and African culture, the first thing they did was that they renounced their identities that separated them from each other. They became Christians as a mystery (Eph 3:1-6). It was so because they all became members of one body in which Jesus is the head. Church was the first inter-cultural association, which upheld the value of equality of all.

It is sad that in the Indian Church, the cultural and caste differences, which deny equality among the members, is persisting. This is untenable to the gospel of Jesus. If the church has lost its ability to ensure equality then it is not a church at all. This calls for a rearranging of our priorities.

3. International Solidarity

Christianity is the pioneer in creating solidarity and support among people who are divided by national boundaries. Jesus in his teaching through the "Good Samaritan" story proved that a Samaritan and a Jew who are culturally and nationally divided are in fact related to one another. The apostles who followed the teachings of Jesus proved that it is possible to love people who are separated and divided in the name of countries and nationalities. When there was a famine in Jerusalem, the Jewish people and Jewish Christians in particular were affected. But, then, St. Paul collected relief materials from Antioch and other nations and sent help (Acts 11:27,30 and II Cor 9:16). It was an act, which was unthinkable on those days. How would you pay your money and share your wealth with foreigners? But the church was the pioneer, which promoted this value of international sharing and solidarity.

Conclusion

The western civilizations were greatly benefited by the Christian values. Love is the core element of Christian values. St. Paul says that there are three great things, they are faith, hope and love, but the greatest is love (I Cor. 13:13). We are living in a world order where people kill others for the sake of faith. For them, faith is the greatest thing. People also kill others for the sake of future hope, as their ideologies justify their action. Foe those ideologies justify their action. For those ideologies, hope is the greatest thing. But St. Paul unequivocally announces that love is the greatest of all. This is what we have seen in the life and mission of Jesus who is the personification of God's love for the world and for all of us. Forgiving the enemy, accepting the alien, as equal and alleviating the suffering of even the 'foreigner' are the expressions of love. This is a compulsion on every Christian.

7. Role of Scripture Teachers

*Rev. Dr. Ipe Joseph**

Some friends are like diamonds. They are forever. They are rare. Jeevan is one. It is a privilege to be asked to contribute an article for the Festschrift being published to honour Rev. Jeevan Babu on the occasion of his *Shashtiyabdhapoorthy*.

It was a great joy to work with Jeevan in the ecumenical areas while we were contemporaries in the our ministry in the National Council of Churches in India (NCCI).

As a pastor, mission promoter, ecumenical colleague, writer and personal friend, Jeevan has impressed all his friends and colleagues. Being present with friends at the time of need is the best of all qualities Jeevan possesses. My wife is of the opinion that, in Jeevan, she always saw a sincere and pious pastor with a sense of humour. As he celebrates his 60th year, we wish him, his wife Kasthuri, and children Keerthi and Kiran a very enriching and joyful time. A special word of congratulation to Adv. Ms. Keerthi Jeevan Babu for the efforts she is making to prepare this memorable volume of her father's life and witness.

I am asked to write on the Role of Scripture Teachers. Scripture teaching is the most important part of faith formation. Jesus has been a great teacher. The three-fold ministry of Jesus–teaching, preaching and healing-puts teaching as important as preaching and healing. Jesus was not only a teacher, but also a learner. He drew his vision and mission from the

Rev. Dr. Ipe Joseph, Former General Secretary of NCCI currently serving All India Sunday School Union, was a friend and colleague, Secretary at NCCI.

scriptures he learned from his childhood from his parents and scripture teachers. He was thorough with scriptures and insisted that we must learn the scriptures and live the scriptures. Scripture provided the guidelines for his life. During temptation, he responded to Satan using the scripture: "Man does not live by bread alone" (Dt.8:3). For other temptations and all major occasions of his life Jesus searched the scriptures for the answer. Even on the cross, his cry was a verse from the scripture; "Eloi, Eloi, lama sabachthani?" (Ps.22:1) So the scripture teacher needs to look up to Jesus as a role model and enable the learners to do the same.

Who are the scripture teachers? Four categories of people are coming to our mind at present : 1) Parents, 2) Sunday School teachers, 3) Day School scripture teachers, 4) Pastors and Evangelists. Parents are the most important of all. Unfortunately, these days parents do not have time for Christian nurture and they do not include it in the priorities of their life. In the day-schools, scripture teaching is restricted. Fifty years ago, the teachers were also evangelists. Now teachers of Christian schools, except in some Roman Catholic schools, do not think of scripture teaching as part of their job.

Pastors also have developed a similar attitude. Most of their time is spent in committees, management issues and court cases. The remaining time is allotted to regular worship services, baptism, marriage, burial and some urgent visits. As a result, pastors do not find time for systematic teaching of the scripture. For many pastors, in their own lives, access of scripture is limited because of the unlimited activities of their profession. So, scripture teaching is left to Sunday School teachers. However, first we will have a quick look at the role of parents as scripture teachers.

Parents as Scripture Teachers

From conception to 3 years, is the most important formative period of human development. The foundations of whatever is basic and significant in human life- physical and mental growth, development of attitudes and aptitudes- are laid during this period. Children are with the parents or guardians at this stage. Some children go to play schools for limited hours of the day. Christian nurturing should begin very early in childhood. Some specific activities can be mentioned here. When the child is able to fix eyes on objects clearly, a picture of Jesus can be introduced into the area of the child's vision. Regularly the parents can draw the attention of the child to the picture saying the name of Jesus. Such a visual aid will enable the child to sustain the concept and image of Jesus throughout life. Another activity is to teach children small choruses, memory verses, and Bible stories. A third activity is to help the children to develop altruistic attitude. This can be initiated through teaching the children to share food, sweets and toys with siblings and friends. When the joint family system was strong, all these things used to happen naturally with the care of the grandparents and other senior members of the family. Now parents in the unit family will have to make conscious efforts in the nurturing of children. Parents will have to allot considerable time to children. There is enough time in this world. It is only a matter of arranging priorities!

Responsibilies of Scripture Teachers

✪   The first responsibility of the scripture teachers is to understand the value of children and develop an attitude like that of Jesus towards the children. They need to make special effort to understand the physiological, mental and spiritual features of each age group and provide effective model of leadership each age group demands. The prominent images are those of mother, teacher, hero, friend, confidant, counsellor and guru, respectively of growing stages.

✪   Motivate the children to love the word of God. The Psalmist says, "How sweet are your words to my taste; they are sweeter than honey" (Ps.119.103). "Your word is a lamp for my feet and a light for my path" (Ps. 119.105). Bible reading cards and Bible notes like IBRA and Our Daily

Bread will help the children to study the Bible everyday of the year. Sunday School teachers should make it a point to constantly remind the students about regular Bible reading and prayer.

★ Interpret the Bible correctly. Bible is perhaps, the most misinterpreted book in the world. Some people follow the literal interpretation. Some others like the exegetical way. Many people look into the Bible to satisfy the desires of their heart, which may be mostly material gains. What does the passage mean in its historical context? What is the message of the passage? How do we translate the message to our situation today? What are the values we need to emulate from the passage? Such questions will help us to effectively interpret the Bible to the learners.

★ Train the children to be sensitive to the situation around them. The scripture teachers should have the Bible in their right hand and the newspaper in the left hand. The Bible becomes meaningful only in relation to our life situation. Life in our community is full of joys and struggles. Sometimes we feel that struggles and pains are much more than joys and well-being. Our world is challenged by poverty, crime, violence, injustice, and threats to life's sanctity. The scripture teacher, using the rich resources of the Bible, will be able to equip the children to respond to all these situations.

★ Pedagogy comes from the word pedagogue (*paidagogos*) – one who helps the children to cross the street holding their hands. The most important role of the scripture teacher is to prepare the children to surrender their lives to Lord Jesus Christ. This does not simply mean a personal commitment only. It means participating in the mission of Jesus in the salvation and transformation of the world in which we live. This means becoming co-workers of Jesus. In this teamwork the scripture teachers and students together make a faithful team, always working in obedience to the Master's call.

8. Role of Science in Spirituality

*Dr. G.S.D. Babu**

From the beauty of the flower in your hands to the grandeur of the stars in the sky, everything in the universe indicates a wonderful order that has been in existence from the beginning of time. But what makes the flower look so beautiful? What gives such brightness to the stars? And many more questions.... The answers for such questions have been the quest of mankind since ages. As the time passed it dawned on man that the universe came into existence with the creation of various laws of nature, beginning with the laws of Physics followed by Chemical and Biological laws.

The first and the most important law may be considered as the law of gravitation, which is the fundamental force that governs the entire universe. The very fact that we are stuck to earth is just because of the gravitational pull that is exerted by the Earth. The paths of the earth and of all other planets in the solar system are strictly adhering to their respective orbits, just on the basis of the law of gravitation. The formation of the galaxies and the stars therein is the result of gravitation. The binding force in the atoms and molecules of all matter also is based mainly on gravitation.

So, who made this gravity? We may name it as law of gravitation pronounced by Sir Isaac Newton. But Newton was not the creator of gravity. He just discovered it. Then came Johannes Kepler who formulated the laws of heliocentric

---

Dr. G.S.D. Babu, currently serving as Director of Birla Institute of Fundamental Research is a close family friend.

planetary motion based on gravity. Of course, he was not the creator of those laws. He was indeed blessed with the ability to understand them and place them in the form of statements.

That was a few centuries ago. More recently, just about a century ago, Albert Einstein gave the famous equation $E=mc^2$ showing the interdependence of energy and mass. At that time, he said,

"I am not looking for the results in any experiment or the causes for those results.

I am only trying to understand the thoughts of the ONE who caused those results."

Now, turn to the passages of creation in the first chapter of Genesis. We see that all the verses clearly show that God gave orders for things to happen. Those orders were nothing but the laws of nature. And only a few chosen men and women like Newton, Kepler, Einstein, etc., were given the privilege to understand some secrets of nature and formulate the appropriate laws in such a way that the rest of the mankind can reap the benefits.

Once the law gets the power from God through such orders, it simply becomes functional. For example, the gravitational force came into existence and applied its influence on the formation of everything in the universe. Likewise, various chemical and nuclear reactions came into being to produce light and heat such as that of Sun and the stars. A more mundane item like water is made with the combination of hydrogen and oxygen under certain conditions. That is, in the absence of these elements and when the conditions are not met, water cannot be made. Same is the case for any other material, like sodium and chlorine for the making of the common salt or hydrogen converting into helium in the Sun as well as in all the stars and going on to make further heavier elements and so on. When such input material is exhausted, the process comes to an end depending again on certain circumstances. Like, our Sun will become a red giant star and then a white dwarf and will be eventually lost into space.

At this point, we may be able to recollect what Jesus himself pointed out about the end of the world (cf. Matt 24.29; Mark 13.24-25; Lk 21.25; Rev 6.12-13; Joel 2.10,30-31). And the astronomers, or the scientists if you may, have been able to show through actual observational studies and applying the knowledge gained through the understanding of the laws of nature, the eventual fate of our Sun and thereby the end of our earth. Thus it is clearly seen that the scientific findings are matching very well with whatever is written in the scriptures.

It may thus be seen that science came into being right at the beginning of creation itself.

As the time passed on, various developments were made based on these laws and we call them inventions, like that of the wheel for transportation, electricity as a usable energy and so on. Further research and the in-depth understanding of these inventions have paved the way for a variety of advancements.

Take anything from your home facilities right up to space facilities, everything is the result of understanding the laws of nature. The global communication system like TV, mobile telephones and so on are all-dependent on the satellites in space. Without understanding the laws of gravity the satellites would not be there in the space. Without understanding the internal structure of the atom and its constituents like electrons and protons, no advancements could have been made in the much-used field of electronics, which has its applications in almost every walk of life.

This is called Technology.

Now, with what God has started as laws of nature, we have been able to reap the abundant benefits from what we call as Science and Technology.

We are clearly aware that all such developments and advancements in science and technology are focused towards the betterment of human existence. These are made by the people who have a deep respect for the laws of nature and thereby for the Supreme Being who created these laws.

But, take the following example. One can use the law called "every action has an equal and opposite reaction" for the purposes of sending rockets to launch satellites for highly commendable purposes like communication, weather reporting, and so on. On the other hand, the same law can be used for making weapons of destruction like guns, etc.

Further, understanding the laws of nuclear reactions that are taking place in the interiors of Sun and other stars can be used for generating power for the good use of mankind. The same understanding can also be used for making nuclear bombs for the destruction of the same mankind.

Thus, one may see that the laws of nature can be focused for good things as well as targeted for evil doings. Such evil deeds are done by those who disregard the Creator of the laws and probably get a thrill out of violating them. They can even argue that such destructive instruments are made for self-defense in the event of an enemy attack. Such arguments can easily be seen as never ending.

In these prevailing circumstances, the scientists as believers in God have been found to be as strong as ever in their faith and confidence in God. There is no clash in their minds regarding the developments in science and technology side by side with their spirituality. As a matter of fact, there is nothing in science which contradicts the faith in God. In fact, it is clearly understood that God is the Supreme Scientist and THE starting point of all science and technology programmes in the entire universe. The ordinary mortals may call themselves as scientists on this earth, who are only trying to get some clues and have been given the opportunity of finding some of them. Surely there is much more in this universe which is still not known to mankind.

I myself had the good fortune of being guided by the Almighty to be an Astronomer and through that had the opportunity of reaching far distances like the icy continent of Antarctica as well the harsh high altitudes in the mountains of Himalayas in the course of my scientific pursuits. Wherever I went, it was for the joy of understanding God's beautiful Universe through the study of stars. And I must confess that I found the laws made by God are being followed meticulously in the entire Universe from the macro size of farthest galaxies to the micro size of the smallest particles of an atom.

9. Fullness of Life and the Role of Life Style

*Rev. Dr. Y. Moses**

I consider it a privilege to write an essay in honour of Rev.Jeevan Babu who is celebrating his 60th birth anniversary. He has always been an inspiring Pastor friend whose unconventional style of pastoral work always impressed me very much. He comes out as a soft spoken and unassuming Christian leader with a deep sense of conviction and commitment about Christian mission. Rev.Jeevan Babu is known for his creativity and unconventional methods of leading people to worship God in spirit and in truth. He also excels as a mentor of several junior pastors. His down to earth outlook of life is evident in all his sermons. I wish him God's blessings as he celebrates his *Shashtiyabdhapoorthy* and would like to wish him a long and happy life.

Lifestyle is a way of life or pattern of life that we follow. It consists of attitudes, values and practices and is determined by life goals. There are as many ways of life as there are goals. And goals are known intuitively and learned in and through community. The repository of life goals of any community is its religion, philosophy or ideology.

Christian community has its own store of knowledge about life goals and life styles, of which the fundamental

---

Rev. Dr. Y. Moses is a Former Executive Secretary of the NCCI. He is currently the Director of the Ecumenical Institute for the empowerment of the Dalits in Bangalore, India and the national coreteam member Safai Karamchari Andolan, a movement for the elimination of manual scavenging.

source is the Bible. The following is a random reflection on fullness of life and the role of life style based on biblical view of life.

The Bible traces the origin of life to God who creates and upholds life in all its fullness or wholeness. There are at least four dimensions to fullness of life, namely, physical, material, social and spiritual.

Physical Life

We often think of physical life only in terms of longevity, although the realists would qualify longevity as reasonable longevity. What is equally important to measure is the quality of life. In fact longevity is dependent on good nutrition and good health care and on good coping mechanism with the given social environment. We are now living in a highly-stressful society and the awareness of the enormity of its consequence has led to a significant development and expansion of mental health-care in our country. There is also an increase in media focus and proliferation of literature seeking to provide guidance to prevent or to cope with stressful and disease situations. While some of it is confusing, there is a general agreement on the need for life style changes. We are rightly advised to adopt a regular regimen of physical exercise and to exercise self-restraint with regard to the types of food that we consume. However the larger question about accessibility and availability of good healthcare and nutritious food to all remains. The vast majority of our people are poor who cannot afford high costs of good healthcare and hence are deprived of the full potential of life.

Material Life

There is some ambiguity with regard to material prosperity in the Christian circles. While some see it as a sure sign of god's blessings others perceive it as a source of evil. A better perspective would promote wealth generation to improve the general standard of life. At the same time it calls for just and fair distribution of the generated wealth.

Prosperity is the opposite of poverty. It can never be built without hard work and expertise. That is why Jesus condemned idleness and indolence while warning against the dangers of wealth. It would be wrong to assume that poverty is equal to godliness, just as it is wrong to assume that all prosperous people are blessed people. Even the wicked prosper. A skewed distributive system also creates and perpetuates high incidence of poverty and growing inequalities.

However, God is pleased neither with the poor nor the rich, but he is with those who do his will. And, of course, God is displeased with the conditions of the poor. Therefore he has compassion for them. Wealth generation is essential, but wealth owners should know that they are only stewards accountable to God. Accumulation of material wealth can never be the key to happiness. Prosperity is never permanent. It can be sustained for relatively longer period by exercising responsibility. According to God's mandate prosperity should permeate to all and for this to happen justice is essential. Therefore it is important to work towards a more just, participatory and sustainable society.

Similarly, there has to be an equilibrium between society, technology and nature. Nature is also a sacrament in which God resides and reveals. Therefore we must lead an integrated life with nature. We must take care of the health of the natural world as well. We should not exploit or seek to dominate, but be stewards of nature.

Social Life

There is an intrinsic quest or inward longing for freedom in all human beings; the desire to lead an authentic life free from the clutches of society. We want to direct our lives, not directed by others or by circumstances. However, freedom and social institutions exist in tension. That is the paradox of freedom. While we seek freedom from restraints of institutions we need institutions (family, state and the church) for acceptance and identity. We are not isolated individuals, but persons in community.

Another paradoxical reality is the conforming tendency of modern man. We are always trying to conform to social groups, be they of any caste, class or region. We have to break free from the oppression of the community/ tradition. We have to overcome the fixation to one's own community and build universal human community.

Spiritual Life

It does not matter how long you live or how you die; it matters where your life would lead you in the end. We are but pilgrims on earth. Therefore, proper conduct of life is important.

Physically, we wish to live longer, materially, we wish to lead a prosperous life and socially, we want a secure and peaceful life. Spiritually we must lead a surrendered life, surrendered to the will of God. Like Jesus, we must be able to pray, 'Not my will but your will be done.'

What is the will of God? What is God's specific will for specific individuals is hard for anyone to lay for another. But it is possible for all to understand God's will in a general way. The evidence in the Bible shows that God desires not only praise and worship with lips, but more fundamentally with actions. Micah has given one of the most beautiful expressions of the intention which God has for all men, when he said, "He has showed you, O man, what is good; and what does the Lord require of you but to do justice, and to love kindness, and to walk humbly with your God?" (Micah 6:8)

Jesus, while emphasising the deutronomic command to love God made it clear that, "You shall love the neighbour as yourself."

Martin Luther maintained that the Christian is a free agent, dominated by no one, yet, under God, the servant of all. The Christian is to enjoy his own external and internal freedom in Christ, but he is to be the servant – literally, a Christ to his neighbour.

The Bible contemplates a double movement – 1) rejection of preoccupation with one's own special personal or group interest, 2) a turning towards the interests of others.

Life styles are conditioned by context and culture. For that reason, at any given context and age, lifestyles interact with each other and influence adherents. Underlying all cultures and lifestyles are principles and values some of which are common and some contradictory. The clash of contradictory values, if ignored inevitably leads to pestering conflicts destroying the very sense of community in any society. Sadly, we are now living in a world full of such conflicts. In our country, caste and communal conflicts are prominent and very destructive. An early resolution of these conflicts is necessary, otherwise they can consume and destroy us much faster than we assume.

Generally speaking, the older generations tend to be culturally conservative, whereas the younger generations prefer life style changes. The young reflect the emerging trends, whereas the older generations are baffled by the same. This is not to say that the young are always right, but when they do and if an imaginative leadership carries them forward, the surge for change is immense and effective. That is what we had witnessed in the 2008 Presidential election in the United States of America. There were some signs of similar surge in India in the aftermath of the recent terrorist attacks in Mumbai. The political class as a whole was unnerved and the promise of a new beginning for clear and fair governance appeared. Needless to say, a similar surge for change within the Indian Church is long overdue. One wonders how and when this would happen.

10. Ecology: Mission of the Church

*Bishop Geevarghese Mar Coorilos**

Introduction

"The human race has, may be, thirty five years left", said David Lyle, in 1969.[1] Lyle's prediction, although slightly exaggerated, has been proved wrong. However, humanity today is still sitting on top of a volcano which can explode any time. It is on the brink of a precipice. Any moment, it could go down into the fathomless depths.

The Context

Creation - Nature is in a state of choas. Earth, which has lost its integrity, seeks renewal. Paddy fields and farmlands have become things of the past. Huge industries and mega developmental projects have now taken over. Arms race and nuclear projects have asumed such an alarming proportion that the very existence of life on the planet is at stake, today. Nuclear projects and other huge developmental projects also leads to a large-scale deforestaion and desertification of land. The devastating impacts of Chernobyl and bhopal on the atmosphere, land and life are still vivid in our minds. Phenomenon called 'Greenhouse Effect' or 'Global Warming'. caused mainly due to the uncontrollable industrialization

---

*Bishop Geevarghese Mar Coorilos is currently serving as the Bishop of Jacobite Syrian Orthodox Church, a colleague, secretary at NCCI and a close friend.

[1]Quoted in Paulos Mar Gregorios, *The Human Presence: An Orthodox View of Nature*, CLS,1980, p.10.

jeopardises the existence of future generations on earth. The ozone layer which is meant to shield us from the lethal ultra-violet solar radiation, has already been considerably depleted. 'Acid Rain' poses yet another grave menace to humanity. Mechanised boats and trawlers devour our marine wealth. Our resources are being fast disslipated. Growing urbanization and the consequent pollutior. of atmosphere degrade our natural environment. Peaceful life on this earth is threatened by the increasing violence incurred both on the planet and its people. Humanity has a great responsibility in seeing as to how far it is responsible for this sorry state of affairs.

A Theological Vision

We need to reflect on the relation between God, humanity and nature. Humanity is poised between God and nature. It shares and unites with God and the world. This is also the meaning of God's incarnation in Jesus Christ. Humanity has been indivisibly united with God in Christ. Because of our focus on this inseparable divine human nature of Jesus Christ, the new humanity becomes a mediating community between God and the world. Humanity, thus gets united with God (Theosis). This, according to Paulos Mar Gregorios, is the meaning of human presence on the earth, that is,to be in Christ, uniting the divine and the human, the transcendent and the immanent; every created entity has an intrinsic worth, and therefore, a right to survive and prosper.

Lynn White considered the Judeo-Christian concept of creation as one of the reasors for ecological crises. According to him, the anthropocentric view of creation in the Bible, combined with the world-view of modern science and technology contributed a great deal to the present environmental impasse. In the Genesis creation account, the Creator accords humanity the freedom to have dominion over the rest of creation. This 'dominion' has been, over the years, interpreted as the license to exploit nature. Although dominion has been given to humanity, it is required to exercise the dominion in the spirit of kenosis, in the way Jesus Christ exercised his dominion (lordship), that is, by emptying himself of all dominion and privileges for the sake of others. Likewise, humanity also must exercise its dominion by being responsible towards nature. Moreover, God entrusted humanity with the task of "tilling and keeping the earth" (Gen 2:14). It is also in this sense that God shared the diving image and likeness with humanity. But human beings have distorted this image and likeness by misusing the dominion, exploiting the earth and its fullness. The root cause of the present ecological crisis can, thus, be attributed to human greed which prompts him/her to enslave and spoil other creations.

Creation is the way of God being with us. God is with us in all compositions of life. The divine presence is beheld in the showers of water, majesty of trees, fragrance of flowers, beauty of meadows, sweetness of fruits, in strong and vigorous winds, and in all movements of life. God said; "Let earth appear". And it was so. Therefore, the earth becomes a theological category for - us the place of our salvation - the vicinity where God incarnated (the act of God becoming earth) in Jesus Christ. Earth is also a liturgical reality. We do celebrate the earth, for instance, through harvest festivals.

The word 'earth' occurs at least fifteen times in the first chapter of Genesis. It suggests that the earth enjoys a unique place in the divine will and purpose. God in Jesus Christ inaugurated the Kingdom of God on this earth and it awaits its fulfilment. Then it becomes a new earth. As Samuel Rayan says, "earth is God's daughter and the creation accounts evoke in us the spirit of a birthday celebration."[2] According to Rayan, the earth belongs to God, for it is God's self-revelation. It is the medium through which the divine uses to address us. The earth is also a sacrament, It convinces us of God's heart, mercy, compassion and power. It is as part of this sacramental dimension that we celebrate festivals. We submit to God, as

---

[2]Quoted in George Mathew NalunnakkaI, "The Earth is the LORD's...*A Reflection*" in *Saplings*, UTC Magazine, Bangalore, 1990- 1991, p.26.

humble offerings, the blessings which we receive from God through the earth.

The nature poet Wordsworth said; "Therefore am I still a lover of meadows and the woods. And mountains and of all that we behold from this green earth "

The book of Psalms also seems to be sharing the same festive mood. It brings to us the spontaneous overflow of powerful feelings such as joy, sorrow, repentance and thanksgiving. Psalm 24 expresses such feelings.

Dominion of God, the Creator over the created order is the principal theme in this particular Psalm. The first verse affirms that the earth and its fullness belong to Yahweh, and to Yahweh alone because Yahweh founded it on seas and rivers, conquering the chaos. This is a recurrent theme in the so-called enthronement passages. It is doubtful whether the Hebrew 'tabel' ('world') is a poetic synonym of 'eretz' ('earth'). Most probably, it is the cosmological dimension which is insinuated here. Rivers and seas are most likely, part of the cosmic waters upon which the earth is established. If earth and its fullness belong to God,- it naturally follows that it's inhabitants share the resources equally. Why, then, is wide disparity experienced today? Human greed makes rest of the creation serve its insatiable wants. Even among human beings, it is only a minority who enjoys the bulk of earth's resources. In India, about 40% of its population has hardly any land or wealth, whereas the top 10% owns more than 60% of me land. The idea of establishing a realm of dominion, namely private property, is somehow fostered into our culture. Identity and Status are being determined vis-a-vis what one has, not in terms of what one is. The inequalities prevailing in the distributive and ownership pattern are a clear distortion of God's image in us.

Church's Mission

The Church needs to ponder over as to how far it has helped in perpetuating this inequality. In this connection, it may be worth taking note of the words of an African delegate at the Nairobi Assembly of the World Council of Churches. He said, "when missionaries came to our land, we had our land with us and they (missionaries) had Bibles is their hands. When they left us, we had their Bibles in our hands and they had our land." It looks as though the Church has lost its genuine missionary vocation. It may also be worthwhile looking into the views of the early Christian thinkers and fathers counted it as common property. Samuel Rayan summarises them as follows:[3]

a) Earth is the gift which God gave humanity in this world. Early Christian thinkers and fathers counted it as common property.

b) Private ownership, concentration of land and accumulation of wealth which leaves others dispossessed and impoverished involves fraud, robbery, plunder, and injustice.

c) Private property is the root cause of all kinds of conflicts and disharmony.

d) Private property is idolatry.

e) They upheld a system which stands against private ownership and which advocates common ownership of resources (We find similar views propagated in Acts 2 and 4).

In short, if we hold on to the theological position that the earth and its fullness belong to God alone, then, it is also the divine will that the resources are equitably distributed among human beings.

Eco-justice

The real victims of environmental blights are the poor and the, marginalised sections of society. The very fact that the ecological crisis is the fallout of the existing capitalist and

---

[3]*Ibid.*, 27.

lopsided development paradigm, makes it a people's concern. It occurs out of the exploitative structures where the rich and the powerful exploit resources unjustly. In other words, social injustice, and environmental degradation go hand in hand. It follows, then, that eradication of poverty can only be possible when environment is well taken care of. There seems to be emerging a new awareness that environmental problems are not just the results of social injustice, especially poverty, but that poverty is also caused by environmental degradation often carried out for the sake of the so-called 'developmental projects'. For example. when the rainforests are destroyed to make way for nuclear plants or huge dams which would only benefit the industrial sector and the urban rich, it is the poorer sections of the society, particularly the tribal people, who live in close proximity with the forests, the fisherfolk, among them their women who have to pay a heavy price. Or when the cultivation of staple food is replaced by cash crops, as happens in India today at an alarming pace, it is the traditional farmers and landless labourers who have to suffer the consequences. Hence there is an inextricable link between penvironmental degradation (alienation from nature) and social and economic marginalisation of basic communities (alienation of peoples).

Concern for the earth and commitment to the poor are held in balance in the Jewish tradition which is very well expressed in the institutions of *sabbath* and *jubilee year*. It is not just human beings (labourers) who require rest, but nature (land) as well. Ex.23:10-12 blends these concerns:

> For six years you shall sow your land and gather in its yield, but the seventh year, you shall let it rest and lie fallow so that the poor of your people may eat... refreshed.

Besides affirming the integrity of creation, the passage also brings out the link between the survival of the poor and the sustenance of land. This suggests that only by protecting the environment can the problems of the poor be redressed. The Old Testament prophets also upheld the interrelationship between social justice and ecological balance. According to them, one of the reasons for environmental hazards was the sumptuous lifestyle of the rich. Joel J., for instance, had no doubts that the rich with their extravaganza would be punished by the earth for exploiting the poor and the environment. He said:

> Alas, for the day...Is not the food cut off from our eyes... the seeds shrivel under the cloud, the granaries are ruined (Joel 1:16-18).

Isaiah was even stronger in his denouncement of the wastefulness of the rich when he said:

> Ah, you who join house to house, who add field to field... For ten acres of vineyard shall yield but one bath (Is.5:8-10).

Book of Job contains some of the richest eco-justice insights. Job, when he gets out of his self-piety, realises the solidarity he shared with other creation in pain and suffering. The 'Speeches of Yahweh' go beyond the human factor in meeting justice which is so well exemplified in chapters 39 to 41, giving at the same time, a clear admonition to humanity that they should not be pre-occupied with their concerns in isolation from those of nature. The cry of the oppressed and the travail of nature are one and the same. This makes the 'integrity of creation' a socio-political, and therefore, a theological concern.

Eco-Spirituality

In traditional Christian theology, humanity becomes the sole object of God's concern. The cosmos is excluded from the purview of salvation. We need to develop a new life ethic, a new spirituality which would converge social and ecological justice. Eastern religious traditions, by and large, express harmony with nature. The underlying theological principle is that of panentheism. Hinduism, the predominant religious tradition in India, is considered by many scholars as a panentheistic religion as opposed to the popular view of

Hinduism as a pantheistic religion. There is no dichotomy between the spiritual and the natural. Likewise, Taoism sees cosmos as an organic interconnected system. As Ian Barbour points out:

> Every particular being is a manifestation of the Tao, the nameless unity that exists before differentiation into multiplicity.[4]

The Taoist concept of 'wu wei' does not imply nature in static form, rather it denotes action that is in tune with the true nature of things. Humanity is part of a wider cosmic order and it should respect the rhythms of nature.

Zen Buddhism which is a confluence of Taoism and Mahayana Buddhism also underscores human kinship with nature. In the Zen tradition, nature is to be contemplated and appreciated rather than mastered. Nature is accorded an intrinsic worth and hence humanity is required to exercise restraint in acting upon it.

The Orthodox theological notion that the earth is sanctified and given as a gift from God to humanity is a powerful assertion. Depiction of earth as 'sacred' in itself can well slip into pantheism (as happens sometimes in Hinduism or in such strands as Creation Spirituality Movement). Creation *per se* is not divine or sacred. It is, on the other hand, sanctified by God, and therefore, entails respect and care. In the Orthodox tradition the sacraments and the liturgy have immense ecological significance. The use of natural resources like incense adds a 'natural' and an environmental dimension to worship. The liturgy for Palm Sunday is of particular importance. The prayers offered in this liturgy are not just for human beings but for the whole creation. Earth is delineated as a theological category, the medium of incarnation (God became

---

[4]Ian Barbour, *Ethics in an Age of Technology*, The Gifford Lectures, Vol. 2, S.C.M. Press Ltd, London, 1992, p.72.

'earth' in Christ) and the locus of our salvation. The ecological message contained in the observance of harvest festivals where people offer back to God the gifts of nature is also very profound. This spirituality should also be a 'worldly-ascetic' spirituality which is neither an escape from the world of realities, nor consumerist, but a 'simple' one (in the sense of 'anti-consumptionist' where people take from nature only for their needs and not for their greed). It must also be a spirituality which is rooted in solidarity with the oppressed, the dalits, the tribals, women of these communities, and their ecology in India. This eco-spirituality will correct the elitism of certain religious and theological stands on ecology which focus on a return to the 'original state of the garden'. An integral eco-spirituality cannot and must not be a journey backwards to the garden of Eden, but it ought to be a journey forward to the paradise, to a 'new heaven and a new earth,' the Kingdom of God where peace, justice, and the integrity of creation will reign in abundance.

Let me conclude with the words of the poet-philosopher Kahlil Gibran:

> It is in exchanging the gifts of the earth that you shall find abundance and be satisfied. Yet unless the exchange be in love and kindly justice, it will but lead someone to greed and others to hunger. For the master spirit of the earth shall not sleep, peacefully upon the wind till the needs of the least of you are satisfied.[5]

---

[5]Kahlil Gibran, *The Prophet*, Book Palace Publishers, New Delhi, pp. 44-45.

11. Conclusion

Kiran and Keerthi

We consider it as a great privilege to gift this festschrift in honour of Rev. D.S. Jeevan Babu our father, to thank God and you for your contributions to his life and to celebrate his life and ministry. We know him for two decades. He gave us freedom to think and act. He did not talk too much but he demonstrated in and through his life all he believed and enabled us to pick up beautiful values. We have a very sincere and compassionate mother who complemented our father in all respects. There were no contradictions in them. It is this harmony of values in our parents made us as we are today. They sacrificed their life for us to grow as good Christians and good citizens of India which can be seen in the professions we have taken, as social worker and lawyer. They did not teach us but showed us in their life what it means to be truely spiritual. They led a very simple life through which they showed us to respect life.

My father believed in the gift of life and went through of all its shades and celebrations with thanksgiving to God. He did not forget his past in the midst of middle class city life due to his status and profession today. God has endowed him with so many talents. He worked hard on his preaching and communicated God's word beautifully. He loves music very much both listening and singing, particularly Indian classical and the old film songs. He loves to read to keep himself updated in biblical knowledge, theology and current affairs in the world. He did not waste time. He used his time in reflections and putting his reflections in writing. He is a workaholic. We, the family members never went for a holiday more than two days during the last 30 years. He relates himself with people beautifully and never gets angry with anybody. He respects elders, encourages the youth and loves children. He is an admirer of beauty. He has good number of friends throughout the world who love and respect him for his humility and humane approach to life.

If everyone had such a father, a really good dad like our, the world would have been so much better.

It is for these above reasons we thought it is appropriate for the family members to present this festschrift. Hope you will find this volume helpful as some of his friends who occupied prime positions have reflected on the theme LIFE IN ALL ITS FULLNESS in spite of their busy schedules.

ENJOY LIFE AND ENABLE OTHERS TO ENJOY LIFE IN ALL IT'S FULLNESS.